To Priscilla,

Shine the Light for all to see
Glow & Grow!
Shine On Shine On
Life is Renewed again!
The Angels of Life

Christni 07/2011

Angel Talk

Chatting with the Angels

Messages given to:

Christine Sabick

From the Angels

ANGEL TALK/CHATTING WITH THE ANGELS

Copyright © 2010 by Christine M. Sabick

Angel Talk / Chatting With The Angels. All Rights Reserved. No part of this publication may be used or reproduced or transmitted in any manner what so ever, including Internet usage, without written permission from the copyright/publisher, except in the case of brief quotations embodied in critical articles and reviews.

The author of this book does not dispense medical advice or prescribe the use of any technique as a form of treatment for physical or medical problems without the advice of a physician, either directly or indirectly.

The intent of the author is only to offer information of a general nature to help you in your quest for emotional and spiritual well-being. In the event you use any of the information in this book for yourself, which is your constitutional right, the author and publisher assume no responsibility for your actions.

First Edition   First Printing, 2010

Book Design and Layout by: Christine Sabick - assistance from Gary Hopkins

Cover Design: by Gary Hopkins   (www.findingsource.com)

Photography of Author by: Amanda C. Pasman

ISBN: 1451521499   EAN-13-9781451521498

Printed in the United States of America via Create Space.com

Publisher: Christine M. Sabick

Dedication

Angel Talk is dedicated to all those who have taken up their shields and have answered God's call to bring Light to the World.

To the Angels who have organized this Army for God and who have given me these wonderful words to share with others.

My wonderful sister and friend, Kathleen M. Vanosdol walked down the path into the amazing Healing Garden where Jesus sat, on January 26, 2010. Jesus held out his hands and said to her, "Come along with me!" She is now healed from cancer. God will always hold you in his arms. We love you and will miss you here but will meet you on the other side of life one day. Your life and kindness blessed so many!

Frances A. Daniels, my daughter-in-law's mom, the Angels took her for a flight home to God on January 2, 2009. You were right we are family and you will be missed here in the physical.

Rev. Douglas Balzer made his transition home on November 8, 2009. Fly with the Angels and write home once in awhile!

To my good friend Theresa Mayhugh, who has been home in spirit for several years but still thought of. You have been along for this journey just as I promised!

Table of Contents

Page#

Acknowledgments 14-16

Author's Photo & Biography 17-19

"Happiness and Smiles" by: Olivetta Nov. 2009......................... 20

Credentials.. 21

My Mission Statement 22-23

Preface.. 24

SECTION ONE: Personal Growth with the Angels 26

"Shine, Shine, Shine" by Madrina Dec. 25, 2005 27

Prelude with the Angels.. 28

SECTION TWO: Personal Messages from the Angels............ 42

The Beginning Communications with the Angels

"Create Within" by: Madrina 43

Why Another Book and Why Me? 45

How Did I Receive the Gift to Hear the Angels? 51

How the Angels Messages Began... 54

First Angel Message... 57

Encouragement... 59

God's Perfect Gift... 60

TABLE OF CONTENTS

SECTION TWO: (cont.)

Are We Alone? 63

Tending Your Garden of Life 67

Handling the Annoyances in Life with Inner Peace 68

People and Their Insensitivities... 70

People Are Good.. 73

Celebration of Life... 76

Looking Through God's Eyes 77

What is Meditation? 78

What is the Purpose of Meditation? 79

Why Should I Meditate? 81

SECTION THREE: Questions Answered by Angels 88

"Waiting" by Madrina July 18, 2008 89

Are The Angels from God? 91

Can Anyone Talk to the Angels? 93

How Many Angels Are There? 94

The Angels Answer Friends Questions 96

ANGEL TALK/CHATTING WITH THE ANGELS

SECTION FOUR: The Angels Speak Out.......................... 140

Various Angels speak about their topic of interest

"Angels of Mine" by Madrina Feb. 23, 2009 141

Angel of Abundance... 144

Angel of Prosperity 148

"The Colors of Life" by: Madrina 152-153

Angel of Knowledge... 155

Abundance with the Energy Ball of Light................................... 160

Angel of Poverty... 162

Angel of Abundance about the Law of Attraction...................... 164

Angel of Humor.. 171

Angel of Compassion.. 174

Angel of Peace.. 176

Angel of Peace and Joy... 177

Angel of Transformation... 180

Angel of Happiness... 183

Angel of Fear.. 188

Angel Blessing 191

Angel of Patience.. 192

Angel of Trust... 194

Angel of Faith 196

TABLE OF CONTENTS

SECTION FIVE: Universal Angel Messages 202

"The World" by: Madrina 2003 203

Changing The Way the Universal Energy Flows 204

Christmas Message 210

GOD 213

Passion For Life 221

A Troubled World 222

Help In Troubled Times 225

Group Consciousness 227

The Shift That Happens 229

God's Energy In Motion 231

Kind and Gentle Reminders 233

Trapped in Life 234

Fate, Karma and Free Will 238

Wake Up and Do God's Work 240

Freedom 242

Emotions 243

"Calling The World Angels" by Olivetta July 10, 2002 249

ANGEL TALK/CHATTING WITH THE ANGELS

SECTION SIX: Working With Your Creative Angels 262
"Dream" by: Olivetta   Dec. 1, 2009 263
Introduction to the Creative Angels 264
Angel Poetry 267
Notebook from 2002-2004 Crossover Experiences............................ 275
Gift of Healing/Angel Crystal Grid Work 281

SECTION SEVEN: Angel Experiences.................................... 286
"Angel Divine" by: Madrina   April 9, 2009 287
Last Section – Right Now Begins the Rest of Your Life 298
Angel's Interaction at Transition Time 296
Gail's Angel Experience 303
Abuse of the Angels? 305
Shelby and Ethan's Angel Experience 308
God Sends People into My Life 310
New Adventures 320
Angel's Ending Comments.. 338
"Shine On" by: Madrina 332
Referrals... 337
Spiritualist Organizations in the United States 338-339
Recommended Reading 340

TABLE OF CONTENTS

Meditations and Assignments

Section Two:

1st Assignment: Relax, Breath and then Smile............................. 65

Meditation #1: Melting Hatred with God's Love 85-86

Section Three:

2nd Assignment: Talking With Your Angel 131-133

Meditation #2: Meeting Your Personal Angel...........................136-139

Section Four:

Meditation #3: The Light and Feeling of Prosperity 151-152

Meditation #4: Warming of a Happy Heart 185-186

Meditation #5: Receiving messages from specific Angels 200

TABLE OF CONTENTS

Section Five:

3rd Assignment: Prepare for the Angels and Let Go of Blocks 218-219

4th Assignment: A Release Technique ……..………………….. 245-248

Meditation #6: Expanding Your Consciousness ……………… 258-260

Section Six:

Meditation #7: The Light of Abundance …………………........... 284-285

Acknowledgments

This book has come about because there are so many friends and family members who have given me their support and encouragement over the years.

Topping off my Thank You list is my husband and friend Stan. I am grateful for all of your support and encouragement. For the time that you gave up being with me, so I could go off for my studies and for the time away to write!

He is the love of my life and my best friend. Our married life of thirty-four years and counting is a fantastic blessing. Thank you for the encouragement to accomplish these things in life and the encouragement to bring about the completion of this book!

Next on my list would be our children who have been there for us through thick and thin! We have all had so many fun times which have held us together through the tough times. It is great to have such wonderful children to share life with, through the laughter and tears. Thank you so much for keeping the faith in us.

I send my love to our son Stanley, his wife Brandy, our granddaughter Shelby, our daughter Amanda, her husband Greg, our grandsons, Ethan and Quintin, our daughter Natalie, and our youngest son Ian.

ACKNOWLEDGMENTS

What a blessing family is and ours is so special. I am sure our family will continue to grow and each new addition will be welcomed with open arms and kept in our hearts. Our children and grandchildren bring a sparkle to our eyes and so much joy to our hearts.

I wish to tell all of my family members that I am so grateful for their friendship and love. I would like to especially thank my mother and father for their love, all the years of their belief in God and sharing that journey with each of us.

To my friends, students and teachers who have inspired me over the years I send you gratitude for touching my life with joy, laughter and life memories. This includes all of my fellow students from USCL, Camp Chesterfield and Lily Dale, whom I have met through my many years of studies. I thank all of the many teachers who have inspired me. You have all been such a wonderful blessing to me along the way. I am grateful for your friendship and the support that you have given to me.

To all those wonderful friends and family members, who have shared their own Angel stories or questions for this book, you have warmed my heart with your faith. Without you the book would not shine as bright!

Gary Hopkins is a fantastic person and friend. I am blessed for having met him. He came to my rescue by putting so much time and energy into helping me with the book.

I want him to know how much I appreciate all of his help pulling this together and producing such an awesome cover design!

To Connie Schultes, Sherri Sink, Brenda Goetz, and my husband Stan, I want you to know how much I appreciate the time each of you have put into reading this manuscript, checking for any mistakes and giving your feedback about the book.

I would love to mention every person by name, but there are so many who have influenced me to write this book over the years. They have given me their support and believed in me, when I probably did not believe in myself, as much as I should have.

To all of those people who attend the United Spiritualists of the Christ Light Church and those who had attended the former Spiritualist Church of Light and Hope, I would like to say thank you for touching my life in such a special way.

Thanks to my friends Rick Webster and Ron Bradford for the computer help, when transferring the files for the book.

BIOGRAPHY

Author: Christine M. Sabick

Cincinnati, Ohio

Angel Talk / Chatting with the Angels is Christine's first book.

Photography by: Amanda C. Pasman

Biography

The Angels have worked so much in my life over the years. When talking about this topic, I am not really sure where to begin. One thing that I am sure of is that the Angels will direct me just fine!

Talking with the Angels and knowing they were around seemed to happen to me since I was a little girl. When I was growing up I could remember seeing Angels around other people. I could also see what they were doing with the people. Many times they were just gently leading them along in life. Other times they were picking them up and carrying them along the way. There was always this wonderful energy of light radiating from them.

Once I grew into adulthood I started to hear them calling to me. I could hear them asking me to speak for them and write their words down for others to see. I knew they were calling louder and louder over time.

The draw to study the healing methods came about and so I began to take as many classes as I could find. I began to see things when I was working with people in the healing modalities. There were grids of lights and surgeons coming in to work on my clients.

BIOGRAPHY

Over the years the Angels gave me a wonderful healing modality that they called, "The Angel's Crystal Grid Work".

The Angels have assisted me in developing several classes of Spiritual development and meditation, including the "Angel Talk" class.

Through the journey to study Mediumship I was guided to become a minister. This adventure took me on a journey of a little over a 9-year span of learning. I finally finished and became an Ordained Spiritualist Minister and the Assistant Pastor of the Spiritualist Church of Light and Hope, in Cincinnati, Ohio. During this time as Assistant Pastor I worked on developing an excellent program to teach others Mediumship Development.

It was announced the church would close in May 2009. Now my journey opens new doors of opportunities. I continue to study and learn as I go.

Currently I serve as one of the Directors of Ministry and the Director of Education at the United Spiritualists of the Christ Light Church. (USCL) www.uscl.org.

"Happiness and Smiles"

When you smile from within, you light up the world.

Happiness grows with each lift

of the ends of the lips and a twinkle of the eye.

Inside and out, grow and glow.

Let the heart sing.

Allow the glow to escape

from the depths of the cave within.

Light up the sky

with a song from your heart.

Finding your smile, finding your smile,

shines great happiness.

Olivetta   **November 2009**

Credentials

Licensed by: the Ohio Medical Board- in 1986 for Electrolysis and began Laser Hair Removal in 2000.

Certified Medium Missionary: at USCL, United Spiritualist of the Christ Light Church; began studying in 1998; was certified in 2002; began my studies at Camp Chesterfield in 1997; certified in August 2004.

Ordained Minister: through the Indiana Association of Spiritualists/Camp Chesterfield on October 28, 2006.

Certified Healing Touch Practitioner: October 1997 after beginning study in 1993.

Reiki Master/Teacher - Usui Shiki Ryoho Reiki and Traditional Reiki: Began studying Reiki in 1997 with various teachers and became a Reiki Master/Teacher in May 2001 and have been teaching Reiki classes since June of 2001.

Certified in Reflexology: February 2004 after beginning study in 1997.

Certified AngelSpeak Facilitator: April 2001, presently teaching Angel Communication and Angelic Crystal Gridwork Healing.

My mission statement is:

- To touch as many people's lives as I can.

- To help people feel more confident in themselves.

- To help people to become empowered to live the best life they can.

- To find ways to help lift people up higher everyday! Smile & be Happy!

- To Promote Spiritualism and the values of this faith. This is a faith that I cherish to the core of my being. It has changed my views on life and the way I live it.

- I hope to inspire others to explore their path to find their connection to God, their higher spirit and the peace within.

I teach Angelic Healing (Intuitive Healing) & How to Communicate with your Angels, Reiki, Mediumship Development and Meditation.

There have been many opportunities where I have worked with families and friends on healing from grief with the loss of loved ones.

MY MISSION STATEMENT

I work directly with those making their transitions to help the person feel more at peace at that time in their life.

When I am called home to fly with the Angels, my goal is to leave behind a legacy about the teaching of how to accomplish belly laughter. This is laughter which grows from the very core of your being and in turn produces a great big smile!

Laughter is the best medicine around! You can not beat it for the best healing you can get!

I would also like to leave these words from the Angels behind so others can receive the uplifting feelings from them, just as I have had over the years.

Preface

Okay, grab your cup of coffee or tea, get ready to sit back and relax and have a chat with the Angels.

I was told that I was going to write a book! I said yeah sure ME? I really did not know what the book would be about but that nagging feeling was there. I just knew somehow it was meant to be.

I heard a voice one night while writing in my journal. The Angels told me that a book was necessary. They asked if I would take the time to sit and write what they wanted to say. I said, okay. I took up a pen and with many notebooks, began this journey over the last fifteen years. I am watching the adventures as they unfold in my life every day!

When I was asked what I would write about they said, "**Angels work in everyone's life! Write about Angels and our work. Get people to see and feel us, then your work will continue to succeed! Make a list of things in your life you feel Angels help with. Angels are God's helpers and we are here to help! Just ask and we will fly with you and help in God's name dear children!**"

I did make my lists and now it is your turn! Go ahead make your list and begin your journey with the Angels. Let it all start from here!

PREFACE

Personal Growth

With The Angels

SECTION ONE

"Shine, Shine, Shine"

"Oh wonders from above, how would you see the light?

Shine, Shine, Shine…..

Open your eyes and see the wondrous light from above.

See the light shine from the eyes of so many…..

See the God in all.

The Glory of God is at hand, The Glory of God is here.

Know that the light is not far away

It is just beginning to glow from above

and lighting the hearts of many.

See the light….Watch it grow….Watch it glow bright.

Hang on dear ones…. Hang on,

It will shine so brightly for everyone to see.

Watch dear ones and see."

Madrina   Dec. 25, 2005

Prelude with the Angels

January 24, 2004

"Christine, the first day many years ago when you became aware of us, we were working with you on your journey to bring you to this place in life. We are still working with you, guiding you on your path because you asked.

Remember to tell people that just because they ask for our help, things may not come back exactly as they asked. We only give what we know to be of the highest good for the person who asked.

SECTION ONE: PERSONAL GROWTH WITH THE ANGELS

> Sometimes it may take time to bring things about. First we must ready the person and then we can bring the answer about.
>
> People must always keep God in their hearts and in their lives. This energy no matter what the people call it, is a God energy above all else. By working with both sides of this energy many things can and will occur."

From the Angels of Wisdom and Light

This is the ending of the year 2009 and this message still rings true. I know that the Angels have been sent from God to help me along the way. I also believe that they are working for God to help us and this is what they have to say about this today:

> "We really want every human being to know that God is sending us to each of you at this time to help with your lives. We want to have people hear us and take time to acknowledge that we do still exist. We have come to you at this time to help each of you to become more aware of us so that we may assist you with your Spiritual development."

This book is to help those who need a reminder that things in life can get in the way of us actually living our life. We sometimes have a habit of letting life just slip on by and we get caught up in the rat race of every day things.

The Angels ask, when this happens, try to find some peace inside yourself and then decide that you can just be happy, regardless of what is happening in your life.

The Angels wanted me to show you through my life, that you can get so caught up in life, you might allow some opportunities to pass you by, or if not pass you by, to be put on hold.

I know that I have put off writing this book because I allowed life to get in the way. I always thought once I get this finished or that accomplished or I get things organized in our house, I would have more time to write what the Angels are asking me to write.

Sometimes, I thought I was not sure the messages would mean anything to anyone else. I felt these messages were for my life. I just did not understand that these messages would mean anything to anyone or that I actually had anything to say.

Well, maybe I do not have anything to say, but the Angels tell me that they do and if I would just put this all together in a book then it will help others.

So, here I am years later composing these messages and gifts that I have received from the Angels, into the book I promised I would do so many years ago.

They want me to explain that even though we do get caught up in the life events, they will still travel beside us and never leave us alone.

SECTION ONE: PERSONAL GROWTH WITH THE ANGELS

They ask that you never, never, never doubt that you do have an Angel flying right beside you and that they are taking care of God's most precious cargo....YOU!!

July 26th, 2004

Okay Angels, please talk to me and tell me what I need to know about all of this! Please......

> "Oh dear Christine, do you not know by now that we have you in the palm of our hands. We do not leave you alone at all. We are carrying you higher and higher.
>
> There are many lessons to learn here and one of them was today. Remember to smile inside and out and carry a grateful heart for all things. No matter how upsetting they may seem. Always remember there is a bright spot in each and every day. Sometimes you might have to look a little harder, some days a lot harder, but it is always there.
>
> Never say or think I can not do it! You always can! Do not put up those types of barriers, there is no stopping you now! Do you not understand that? Just keep moving forward, you are progressing every day!
>
> We ask that you keep your light shining bright. Do not put it out. Others need to see and hear so much of what we want to teach.

This is just one example that you need to bring out to let others see how God is in their lives through all things.

God will carry you as far as you want to go. There is no desire left unheard. All things are possible with God in your heart. Carry that energy ever so close and do not loose it.

Constantly be in the grateful heart. You will then see the sunshine shining bright.

When you are living in doubt or troubled we will put the ray of sunshine out for you to see. We will hold you in God's arms!

Turn all troubles over to God and let him carry them. Allow that light to shine bright again. You were not made to carry such a heavy burden! God made the promise, that he would carry you forever. So take him up on the offer! Do not be such a control freak, just let God do it!!!"

Love and Light forever and ever and ever!!

Your Angels of God's Light and Energy of Love!!!

I then heard this loud noise go by which sounded like, "Swooshshshshshhhhhhhhhhhh!!!!" I just knew the Angels had visited again.

This entry was the one that I thought helped me to move forward.

SECTION ONE: PERSONAL GROWTH WITH THE ANGELS

I received the title of the book as well as a message that just knocked my socks off! I was not wearing any at the time but, oh well!

I just knew that this was the book and what it was about. I made my commitment to help others the best I could, with God's help.

Life once again brought about some twists and turns for me to ride through. I was pulled into many directions and this took me away from the writings on a regular basis.

I can still hear the Angels sing today, years later and I know I am working toward the higher goals for this work. I can tell you that life does not get much easier once you make this dedication to work for God.

Many obstacles were put in my path over the years, and I was waiting for all of this to be proven to me. Is this real and if it is then why was all of this not working in my life? How could I teach others or tell others what I kept hearing if my life did not get any better and why did all of this disorder keep happening in my life?

I finally realized, that it was working for me. I was just trying to force it to be different than it was. I was trying to make things happen the way I wanted them to work. I thought I was trusting God to bring about the help I needed in my life.

I still believe that I had the trust in God, but I was so focused on trying to make my life work in a way that just was not meant to be. I found that I was missing the point of the Angel's messages.

So one night in August of 2007, when things in life were really getting out of hand, shortly before my life made a very major and traumatic change, I asked the Angels this question.

August 24, 2007

Okay Angels, What is happening now? Where should I be? I do not feel I am there and not sure how to get there!

> "Dear Child, you still have not learned to trust that this is what it is. You hear us but are not applying what you hear. You need to listen to the words and the blessings around you. We know you see things differently and you know we are here with you.
>
> We understand your confusion with this life. Take the time you need to work out the difficulties in your life before you make a heavy commitment to us to work for God.
>
> We have so much to offer and to share. We do not want to take too much time to do so, at this time. You have too much to accomplish yet. Now is not the time to sit and try to listen. You have much on your mind and much on your plate to accomplish. We want to have you write these words and it is not too late.

First you must clear the clutter; next you must reach within yourself and decide that you can do this work. Once you decide this then we will intervene again.

For now it is time to rest and then we will work. You must take time right now to sleep and get the proper nutrition for your health.

We will fly away now and return another time with more messages for the people of God's world. For the Peace you need to have, you must get your rest. Time will be on your side, one day soon.

Things are progressing in a direction that will benefit you and your family now. The tide is turning for you. Know that we are always flying beside you and keeping you with us. We only want the best in your life. Smile and be happy now. Do what is in your heart and you will know what is best for you again.

You have lost sight of the vision due to exhaustion. It will return with much light and we will guide you then. Until then rest and get caught up on the work you need to accomplish."

Your Angels

I was a bit taken back with these words and thought that I really did believe I was focused on all of this.

I have been studying for years and have taken on more responsibility for reaching out to people. I have been accomplishing many things.

I do understand that this was not a punishment because that is not how this works. That is what the Angels tell me. This is a time of rest, a time of rejuvenation, and a time to reset my priorities.

I am told to let things settle down more in my life. That way I will have the energy that it takes to carry on with this work.

The Angels were giving me a period of time to understand what this would all lead to. This would give me the much needed time to get my family and myself ready for it.

So for now, I did understand what they meant about clearing out my life to do this work. I did not really understand about the rest. I guess I can say I had become too busy to accomplish what I was being asked to do.

I was about to find out why I needed more rest and that my questions would be answered as would my prayers. Just not in the way I THOUGHT it should be answered. I discovered that over the next few months, my life would be cleared of all of the clutter.

In looking back over the years, I have found no matter what kind of devastating things go on, I did continue to count on the power of God to get my family and myself through it all.

SECTION ONE: PERSONAL GROWTH WITH THE ANGELS

What a blessing this is for me at this time in our lives to have God be a major part of it all. It has kept me pretty much sane throughout the stressful times.

I know without my faith and the knowledge that the Angels are here and working with me through this, I would not have made it this far in the same way.

I know now I have developed a belief and faith that will never be taken away.

I still have challenges, but I will continue to stand strong in my belief that God is a major part of my life. That goes for the times when sometimes I do not understand why something happens in my life.

I have worked hard to find answers to why devastating things happen in people's lives. At the time this is written it is June of 2008 and I have done more studies since the Angels started asking me to write.

I have just felt over the years a calling to help others grow spiritually and help people develop more confidence. I studied about various ways to grow spiritually in my own way.

I have not taken time to write as often because I have answered God's call in a different way. The road that I have traveled is different than I would have ever dreamed it would be.

I have found that throughout this time, my life was to be changed very dramatically, just as I was told it would be.

I have gone through so many challenges and found that there have also been many changes in my personal life.

My children are grown, have moved from our home and have their own lives. My husband and I moved from the farm and we downsized tremendously.

We basically got rid of all of the clutter in our lives just as the Angels asked me to do over the years. It was a very difficult decision and move, but was necessary for us to go through at that time.

We are now working on moving forward with our lives. My dear husband is such a support for me in this work. He is working right beside me to begin our work doing what the Angels are showing us.

With our children grown and having less responsibility, I finally felt it was the right time in my life to answer the call of ministry. As an Ordained Minister and having been the Assistant Pastor of a church, I found that I learned so much during this phase of my life. I have grown spiritually over the years.

With the closing of the church, I have a calling to write more and work more than ever with the Angels to help others in a different way.

SECTION ONE: PERSONAL GROWTH WITH THE ANGELS

As I begin to look back over my life, I realize that all of the restructuring that was going on was necessary to begin to do what God has asked of me. I did accept this invitation to do God's work many years ago and began putting things into motion to accomplish this.

I now believe that the things that were so difficult to live through cleared the way for me to have the freedom to work for God.

It allows me the time to begin to bring the messages to the people like I was asked to years ago.

Through this changing time in our life I asked many questions and listened to the lessons. I have now come out on the other side of this experience stronger in my faith and with a peace in my heart.

My life continues to be very busy, but still I have a deep seeded call to organize the messages from the Angels and put them into a book. For years I have heard this and now my life has been cleared of the many obstacles that always seemed to be there.

The road is now open for me to finally do just that. This is the right time for the messages I have been receiving to come out to the public. The Angels voices can begin to be heard in the proper perspective.

Of course I hear… FINALLY!!! I hear a little bell, a tinkle of laughter. They say all is in Divine Order and now is when your book is needed. So we write.

I partner with the Power of God, through the Angels, to form the Army that will work from the Heart Center of Love. This will help to shine the light over the entire Universe. It is sending out God's Love to all those in need of God's love and assistance.

I hope through my experiences and the answers from the Angels it will help others get through any difficult times in their lives. Then we all can see and enjoy more fully all of the amazing wonders of life!

The Angels really are out there working hard for God and they desperately need our help!

When things are going wonderful in life or when you are facing obstacles, know that God is helping to direct you on your path in this lifetime.

The Angels are forming an Army for God. Will you be ready and willing to join them in this battle? They are calling out to all! Can you hear them?

SECTION ONE: PERSONAL GROWTH WITH THE ANGELS

Personal Messages From The Angels

SECTION TWO

The Beginning Communications with the Angels

SECTION TWO: PERSONAL MESSAGES FROM THE ANGELS

"Create Within"

"We create within ourselves

All that is possible.

Be alive, Look within

The life eternal begins.

Create the life that is meant to be.

Look within to see the possibilities."

Channeled from Madrina

SECTION TWO: PERSONAL MESSAGES FROM THE ANGELS

"Humor – keep your humor or you will loose everything"

By: Madrina

Why another book and why me?

Several times over the past few years I have asked the question, "Why are you calling me to work for God?" There are so many out there who are doing an excellent job, telling people about Spirituality, Angels, speaking to their loved ones in spirit etc, etc. I have received many answers to this question.

I will now share some of these answers, to help you understand a little more about when you hear this calling or when you just do not know why you are asked to help in this cause.

ANGEL TALK / CHATTING WITH THE ANGELS

February 9, 2009

Today I was at home in bed because I was feeling pretty sick. I just did not feel up to doing much and decided to stay in bed for the day.

You know how it is when you want to stay in bed, things just keep coming into your head on what needs to be getting done around the house.

Letting go of everything, I finally decided to just clear my mind and ask for the Angel of Healing to come to help me sleep and heal.

That was the beginning of a lot of writing for this day. I guess the Angels had other plans for me than bringing sleep my way. I was no longer thinking about all that I needed to accomplish at the house, because now, I just had random thoughts coming into my head.

I finally decided that the only way I would get any sleep was to get a notebook and begin to write again. I could not find a blank notebook and remembered I was going to buy one today. Now I just was not feeling up to getting up out of bed to run to the store and get one. I told the Angels I needed to sleep. I promised I would go out and buy a notebook the next day so we could then write again.

As I lay back down in bed I figured I had made a deal with the Angels and could finally sleep.

SECTION TWO: PERSONAL MESSAGES FROM THE ANGELS

Good try! That did not work, since the same thoughts just kept coming into my head over and over again. These thoughts just would not leave, no matter what I did.

I finally gave in and figured this is just ridiculous because I am not sleeping anyway. I will just get up, find something to write on and get it out of my head.

I found a few pages left in one of my journals; I decided to mark it so I could find it later. I would just write the words down and see what happens.

I started to write, and when it was finished I had 10 pages from the Angels. I guess they really wanted to talk today!

The Angels had been after me for several years to write all of this down in my journals and eventually put it in a book for them. They have also asked me to speak for them to those who chose to listen.

I have asked the Angels several times why I should write another book about what they are saying, since there are so many already published. I even told them that I really was not a writer. The Angels have now answered me by telling me:

> "Just write what we ask and you can write just like you hear us telling you what God wants for your world."

ANGEL TALK / CHATTING WITH THE ANGELS

I heard this next part of the message with such determination in the words that I could not help but understand the importance of what they said.

> "Christine, there are many being called and many writing about us. There are still many people that are not hearing. We need so many more people of God's Light that are willing to tell others that there is help out there for them.
>
> So many people are so busy and cannot take time from their lives to do the amount of work that needs to be accomplished.
>
> We need more help than ever and only these few cannot accomplish this task. Each person who speaks about the Angels can see and hear a little differently to touch more people's lives.
>
> Some people may need to hear a little differently than others or hear more times than others to get the message. We need others to hear what we have to say in so many different ways, that finally one day, all of the people of the world will hear these messages.
>
> You are now lying down with no place to go. You can not do anything but listen and write. We want to talk and be heard."

I just lay back and smiled and gave the Angels a bit of a laugh and said, "Okay I get the picture, I will write the messages and get them out to whoever will listen. Let's Go!"

SECTION TWO: PERSONAL MESSAGES FROM THE ANGELS

Then the Angels told me that one of the most important messages is:

"God loves all people! No matter what! It does not matter here in God's world, what someone looks like or what country they are from, what religion they are or what their political background is.

It only matters that everyone knows that they are loved and cared for! It is time for the world to awaken to this higher energy and know that loving and caring for your fellow man or woman is what matters.

Please! Please! Please! Everyone awaken and look at your world! Look at the others around you through the eyes of God! See the beautiful children of God walking beside you! These are your brothers and sisters! Everyone hold each other in your hearts and let go of this hatred for mankind!"

I see the Angels at this time, crying tears! I heard someone tell us that Angels do not show emotion. I am going to tell you that at this time, the Angels that are fighting for our world show emotion, so we can get the message in a way that will change us forever.

It just touches my heart in a way that I can not put into words! They want so desperately to get your attention about these messages! They are so determined to change the way people treat each other!

They tell me their mission in this is: **"To change the Hearts of all the People of this World!"**

So for now, I will agree that there are plenty of other books and information out there about this topic. I know there will be people who will disagree with what I am writing. I think it is a great thing that we have free will to agree to disagree.

After hearing this last entry and the way it was given to me, my answer for anyone who would like to ask me why I am doing this would be, because I was asked to, plain and simple!

I am writing this book to help those who see, hear or feel the Angels or the spirits of people, to know that it is okay and not to feel different. I hope that this will give you some guidance and support with your growth. I would like for others to not feel so alone. Know there are people out there, who do see what you see and have had similar experiences.

I have long ago accepted that I am different. We are all different from one another! That is a wonderful thing to be different. How boring life would be if we were all the same. So different is good, Right?

Many times I had decided in my earlier years, I needed to stop seeing and hearing the Angels and the spirits from the other side, because it was embarrassing.

SECTION TWO: PERSONAL MESSAGES FROM THE ANGELS

I thought that life would be more normal if I just did not do this anymore. I prayed to God many times over the years about this topic.

I wonder today what a normal life is. Has anyone decided that? Well, I guess that would be different for everyone. What is normal for one could be different for another. So I guess you could say that I am living a very normal life for someone like me!

How did I receive the gift to hear the Angels?

I have always had an ability to hear people say things before they actually said it. Sometimes that proved to be very embarrassing. I would find that I would laugh out loud at something I had heard someone say. Then I realized the words were being said after I laughed about it. I also heard words come into my head that people did not say at all. I decided that it was someone's thoughts. I did not always like what I had heard though.

I do not think I can do that as much anymore and I am glad about that. I really do not want to know all of people's things anyway. I had a friend tell me once that she felt uncomfortable with me sometimes because she was afraid I would know everything about her.

I told her that I have enough of my own things in life to deal with. I just did not need to know everything about her anyway. I just did not go there.

On many occasions throughout my life, I could see people that other people could not see.

I remember when I was in grade school my dad's father told us that he had seen his sister shortly after she had passed into spirit. He told us that she came up the basement steps, stood in the entrance to the kitchen and talked to him, to tell him she was okay.

Well, the basement was where all of us kids would go while visiting our grandparents. Do you think we were all afraid to walk into that kitchen, go down those steps and play in that basement? You can believe that! It was only because I knew one day I would see her standing there and I did not want to!

I just seemed to have a natural intuition about things that were going to happen. I do not know how I could do all of this, I just did.

I had other experiences with my dad's mother. She used to hear people talking all the time and she did see my grandfather's dad the night my grandpa passed into spirit. He came to tell her that he was going to take his son home that night and he did.

I have always had a great love for God and talked to him all the time. I was very aware that I had a Guardian Angel.

I could feel this angel around me and I talked with this presence all the time. I could also get an impression about other people's angels.

SECTION TWO: PERSONAL MESSAGES FROM THE ANGELS

I never thought much of it until I started to tell people about it. One time in high school I freaked some of my friends out by telling them something that had happened. I felt different from everyone else and did not want to tell anyone about it for a very long time. I had decided many times that I would just stop doing this.

When I speak with people about talking to Angels or the spirits of people who have died, some people say they believe this is not from God. They tell me this is from other sources. I did not really believe this, but I did not want to mess with the wrong kinds of things. I finally had to ask God, to please make this stuff stop if it was not really from him.

I even had some nights that I begged God to make it stop, especially when I would see people in our basement. I started to become afraid of it all because no one else I knew could see or hear them talking. It was also because of the possibility that this was not a good thing to do.

I always could see an angel and a bright light when I saw these spirit people. Later when I thought about why I was so afraid, I realized I was only afraid because no one else said they saw the same things as I did. I tried to make myself believe it was just my imagination.

Well, that did not work very long!

I did think that I had successfully put it way back in my mind, but it was still there. I just tried not to pay attention to it anymore.

I finally tried again to make myself believe that I had an overactive imagination!

Over the years, I have said so many prayers about the experiences that I have had and they still do not go away. I have even asked God to take it all away! I can say at this time that if this is not real, I must have one heck of a great imagination. That is for sure!

I finally had to give it over to God and believe that this was actually God's work.

Visions of the Angels are written about throughout the bible. Why would any of us believe that it would not happen today? It is really amazing to me, how many people throughout history label things in the negative, when they just do not understand things nor have an explanation for it.

How the Angel messages began

I was taking a class in 1993 and one of the things they taught us was to take time out of life to take care of you. It was not selfish to do this, but a way for you to stay strong, so then you would be able to take care of others. You needed to work on yourself in a spiritual, physical, and mental way to keep a healthy balance in your life.

I am a mother of four children. I worked hard all day at work and then would come home to many things to tackle before bedtime.

SECTION TWO: PERSONAL MESSAGES FROM THE ANGELS

I had to find some way to take time out for me, so that I could stay strong for my family.

I worked it out that every night I would take time to go to our room to pray for my children, family and the world. This was the best time for me because, my day was finished and the children were in bed. I did not have to think about all of the things I still needed to accomplish. This helped me to unwind from my very busy day.

I would take this time to meditate on things that went on in my day, to get a better perspective on things in my life. This was also the time I would get my mind and notes ready for the following day's work.

I usually started at about 10:00 P.M. and would stay in my room for about one hour every night.

I was learning about journaling in my class and it was one of our assignments. So, I decided to purchase a notebook and started to take some of my hour to write about my day. If I needed to vent about something I usually wrote it in this book.

I would get so involved in writing that my hour would fly by before I knew it. For me this was a form of meditation and prayer time. I was so relaxed that once I was finished, I felt I had accomplished my prayer and meditation time.

One night while I was journaling I was hearing some other words come into my head. I was not sure what it was, but knew it was different than what I had going on in my own thoughts.

I could hear a buzzing sound and felt a slight breeze around me. I decided to start to write what I was hearing.

Once again time flew by and when I was done, I could not remember everything I wrote down. I just could not believe my hour was over. I decided to go back and read what was written in my journal. I could not believe what was written on my paper.

I kept re-reading it thinking, "I guess now I really am crazy!" I thought maybe my day was very stressful and now I really did loose it.

I did not remember writing any of what was there. I know my hand had the pen in it. I know the words came through my head, but then they got lost somewhere. It got to the point that I began to not even hear the words. I only saw them take shape from my hand and onto my paper. I could remember writing but it was not until I was finished and read the words that I knew what was written.

SECTION TWO: PERSONAL MESSAGES FROM THE ANGELS

First Angel Message

I know I had messages many times in my life that I gave to others. I always seemed to talk to people during my life and tried to help. Words just seemed to come into my head to tell them. When I started to write in 1996 it was nice to have something in writing.

My very first Angel message that I actually wrote down came on **August 7, 1996.** This is the message I received that night,

> "I want to tell you I love you with all of my heart and soul. I do exist and I am real. I am your angel helper. My name is Olies, Angel from God of Love. I will take care of your heart and all of your pains. Do not worry about any part of your life.
>
> I am here to help you in any way I can. You will be ready to do the most magnificent things.
>
> I will help guide you in everything you are supposed to do. You will grow and change so much, your life will be so much fuller. You will not believe it now, but believe me, I am truth and honor. Read and Learn Christine! Study!"
>
>   Olies

I was not sure that Angels had a heart or a soul, but hey, that is what I heard, so why question the little things. I will take the message as it was given to me because the message says, I am loved by God.

I listened to what the Angels said about reading and learning. Because as I have said before, that is exactly what I have doing over the last twelve years, learning and taking many classes.

This first message, was my introduction to one of my Angels.

Shortly after this first message, I decided to write some more. I thought I would test the waters to see if this was real. I had to see if I was writing things from somewhere in my mind. I decided to ask a question to see what would happened. I talked out loud a few minutes asking if there really was anyone there. I prayed that I was only hearing from a power of God. I said that if they had a message from God, that they should talk to me and see what we can do from here

That was the beginning of writing for the Angels. I began receiving messages almost nightly. I decided to begin the journaling with my day's events. I would end with a question to the Angels or just say,

"Angels do you have anything to say tonight?"

There have been times when I sat with a pen and paper and just begin to write. I have also written it in a letter format, for example:

Dear Angels,

What do you want to say tonight?

I believe whatever way you want to start your Angel messages is up to you, so ask in your own personal way.

SECTION TWO: PERSONAL MESSAGES FROM THE ANGELS

Over the years I have received many more messages that I will now share with you. I have started to write whatever message the Angels seem to have for me and other times they answer my questions.

The following are just some of the messages the Angels wanted to present to you.

*E*ncouragement

September 6, 1996

My Angel, Olies says,

> "I want you to show love and understanding to all, even yourself. You must forgive all faults including your own. I Love You! I am with you always and I care about how you feel.
>
> When you are upset I hold you always and comfort you. When you are happy I smile and laugh with you! It is time to move forward, be open and ready for the changes in your life. It will be for the good! I say be ready soon, Christine!
>
> Sleep dear one, now sleep!"

They always encouraged me to take care of myself. They say that is the only way I will have the energy to continue to work for them.

This will help me to be able to shine the eternal life of love to others. I know they encourage me to move forward all of the time the Angels say,

> "You must move foreword and not stay still for a long period of time. This is so things do not get stagnant in life.
>
> If you stay in one place and have no movement in life, especially with things you are learning, they become stale and old. We are not asking you to move around or leave your job. It is just that you always need to be alive, growing and learning along the way.

God's Perfect Gift

This next message is for all those who do not think they have anything to offer in this world. The Angels send this to those who do not love and respect themselves or appreciate the gift from God of their lives. It is for those who are sad or thinks no one loves them.

One night late in the evening, I was writing in my journal about the things that went on in my day. I had gained some weight and was feeling a bit down about this. I was always very good at tearing myself down about the way I looked. This was in 1996 at the very beginning of the time that I started to hear from the Angels. They stopped me short in my thinking and the voice came to me very bold and loud.

SECTION TWO: PERSONAL MESSAGES FROM THE ANGELS

These words came to me,

"Christine, God does not make mistakes!"

Then the words softened into words of such love and the message went on.

"God made you in the image and likeness of Himself so how could you be anything less than the perfect gift? They handed me a beautiful box wrapped in an exquisite gold wrap with the most gorgeous gold ribbon on it. God had looked very hard for exactly the perfect wrap and ribbon and once found he put it on this special container. He then filled this package with that which was of great wealth, health, knowledge and wisdom and says that this is all you would ever need in this lifetime"

They then told me,

"Each time you criticize yourself, you are throwing your gift right back in His face and saying no thanks."

You see this beautiful box that was so carefully picked out and crafted with the finest and most exquisite of all the wrapping paper and ribbon and then so delicately put together to make the most gorgeous present ever, was *ME!*

It was me that God took so much care to wrap in this most exquisite package. That touched me so much that it brought tears to my eyes! It still does today whenever I think about this message!

Your life is the most precious gift from God. You need to appreciate it and always live with a grateful heart for all the things that God has provided for you in this life.

Start today to make sure you understand that right now, at this very moment, **you** have everything you could possibly need for this moment.

If you find you are lacking something somewhere in your life, then it is time to stand up, talk to God and ask for direction.

Get yourself motivated to begin moving forward and take action to bring back to you what you already have. That is the ability to make things happen for the better in your life.

God has already given you the ability to move forward in your life. Sometimes it takes making a change that is difficult or letting go of things you think you can not let go of. It does take some sort of positive action on your part to bring about the natural causes of nature in your life. Make decisions in your life to make changes and bring about the positive energy in your life. Be willing to go through what you need to and it will happen.

SECTION TWO: PERSONAL MESSAGES FROM THE ANGELS

*A*re We Alone?

If you feel you are alone this message is for you. It is to give you the strength you need to stand up and feel the Angels with you. This message is being said to bring you the courage to take your first step to go on the avenue of life.

It will help to direct you, to find where you have been and where you would like to go. This will then bring about the ambition to do something about it.

The Angels will carry you and they want you to understand, that you are not a burden on them.

> "We have come to bring you the light, to help light the way and guide you to the understanding that you have the ability to do things beyond your dreams!
>
> Each day when you wake up, you should take time to thank God for a new day. Then watch as your day unfolds, and see all of the blessings that your day holds. You can become more aware of each blessing by keeping a journal. Writing about something you are grateful for at the end of each day.
>
> Begin to write these things down. This way on the days when it is more difficult, you can look back at the list of all that you are blessed with.

> When you lay your head down at night, remember to smile and have a grateful heart, that you were given such a wonderful gift of a new day. This will bring about a new day again tomorrow and bring about the things in that day that you will need. Refresh and become renewed again. Get the proper sleep and nutrition to get through your days."

It is so simple to find something that will get you to smile or something you can appreciate in a day. Look around you and see the trees, flowers, sun shining, blue skies, white fluffy clouds, bird chirping, someone laughing, the wind rustling the leaves, puppies playing, or children laughing. Remember when you were younger all the things that you laughed about, go back in time in your memories and find something good and carry it close to your heart.

I could go on and on naming different things, but hopefully you get a picture of things in your life that can get you to smile through any difficulty. We have been given so much it is up to us to make the most of it all.

1st Assignment: Relax, Breath and then Smile

"So sit back now and relax into your seat. Close your eyes and take a deep breath. Breathe in through your nose and then breathe out through your mouth. Repeat this process three times, each time releasing any tension you might be feeling today.

Think about something that brings a smile to your face.

Focus on this and allow it to become a part of you.

Feel the joy that comes and fills you.

Allow it to bring a peace about you.

Believe it is here with you right now.

Sit with this feeling for a little while and bask in the wonderful beauty of the healing of the Angels of Peace and Joy.

When you are ready, open your eyes and take the feeling of peace and joy with you throughout your day.

Always remember there is plenty more where that came from."

Write down any experiences you may have had in Assignment #1.

SECTION TWO: PERSONAL MESSAGES FROM THE ANGELS

*T*ending Your Garden of Life

I had a day not long ago where I was feeling very vulnerable and having a bit of a pity party for myself. Any one of us can have these kinds of days. I was talking to the Angles about the things going on in my life, when I heard something that reminded me of the song, "I never promised you a rose garden".

I heard the Angels say,

"God may not have promised you a rose garden, but you were given all of the tools and information you have needed to cultivate the ground and the ability to plant all of the seeds which you are given everyday."

When I read this message it made me stop and think, am I using all of the skills I have been given or have learned so far in this life? I do not believe I am! I then made a commitment to do better at utilizing all that I have learned. I can then use this to help others to find more peace. We can all live together in this world that God made for our enjoyment.

*H*andling the Annoyances in Life with Inner Peace

I was having a meeting at my house with some friends on New Year's Eve 2004. We were in a meditation when the front door of my house opens and slammed closed. One of my son's friends came into the house, closed the door too hard and then proceeded to try to come into the room. I felt that this had disrupted the energy, and I became a little irritated at the noises.

When I am by myself these things do not normally bother me. When I am hosting something at my home and have asked others in the house for a little time for quiet, I found I got a bit annoyed. About the time I was feeling this emotion and was not sure I should stay in the meditation, I felt a hand come over my heart. I felt a sudden peace inside me so great that I could not come back yet.

Then a few minutes went by and my dog Elvis, who was in the room, started making noises. He was licking his paws and every time he moved I could hear his claws on the wooden floors.

He just loved being in the room while we are meditating or doing healing. He would always get his feelings hurt if we put him outside the room. I kept trying not to notice all of his noises. He continued to make these noises until I decided this was it, I just could not stay focused any longer. I was sure everyone else in the room was already getting aggravated and ready to come back from the meditation.

SECTION TWO: PERSONAL MESSAGES FROM THE ANGELS

I was just about to open my eyes when I felt a hand on my head and another over my heart. I once again found the peace that I had felt just a few minutes before, only stronger, much, much stronger!

Then I heard the Angels say,

"Christine, all of this does not matter! These are just little annoyances in life. These are all the things that will try to stop you from feeling this inner peace that is so freely given to all! There are so many things in life that come along to try to stop this feeling, some will be little annoying things and others will be more overwhelming.

The little things are not as important as keeping that inner peace. The more overwhelming occurrences that come into your life can be handled better, if you have that Peace already in your heart.

Once you find this Peace deep in your soul, you will have it forever and nothing can take it from you. Look for it, feel and know it exists.

Then you will notice that your eyes have changed, because the way you see things will be different. Before you know it, your mind will change. You will begin to process things in a different manner. You will see and think, Peace!

It will become a part of your whole being, so naturally it will happen, little by little. Then before you know it there, it is PEACE!

Joyous Peace! AHHHHHHH! How nice does that feel? Which would you rather live in, a Hectic, chaotic, rushing world OR have that feeling of Inner Peace?

When I came back from this meditation I realized that the others in the room were just coming back and most of them did not even notice the noises or it did not bother them if they had heard them. I then shared the message that I received in mediation with them.

People and Their Insensitivities

Another type of annoyance at one time in my life, was when I had a problem dealing with people and their insensitivities. It just seemed to me that people were just being so rude to each other or just plain mean when talking about other people. I would sit and listen to others around me and hear what they were saying about their so-called friends.

It just felt so sad and I did not know how to react to this. The more I was hearing the Angels asking for people to find a way to look at people differently, the harder it was for me to hear this happening.

SECTION TWO: PERSONAL MESSAGES FROM THE ANGELS

I found it most difficult because some of these people I had to interact with on a daily basis.

I also found that this negative attitude was flowing over to me. I was starting to see the faults in others and not as much good. I really did not like this, so I asked the Angels what I could do about this and how I could handle this in my life.

Here are a few answers that I heard on this topic:

"My dear, look at each person for their true inner beauty. What you experience with them on the outside is only the journey they are on to learn what they need to learn at this time. If they are put in your path, then take your lesson from that experience because you can be sure there was one. Do you want to miss it again?"

Another time I heard:

"If you walk away when things are difficult or turn your back on something that is not going just the way you think it should be, then you miss out on the adventure of watching things grow into what they could have become!"

July 14, 2008

Tonight I heard the Angels say:

"Dear child, it is important to listen to others and learn from them. When you hear an injustice being done then speak up and try to help others to see the beauty of an individual. Do this in a soft way. Do this in a way that it is not noticeable. Tell them what you admire about someone or what you see as a good attribute of that individual. By bringing in positive feedback you will see others begin to pick up more positive attitudes about others and about life.

This is not always an easy task. Sometimes it is easier for people to go along with the crowd and not make waves. You can do this very subtly. You do not have to come off righteously or better than thou.

You just make a positive point. When you feed others with positivity, then you will grow more positive behavior."

It is time for everyone to work on helping each other to learn more about the fact that we needed to find beauty in everyone and with every experience, no matter what anyone is going through in life, because it all has a beautiful silver lining. Finding this beauty in all things and all people will bring joy, love, laughter and God's light into everyone's life."

The Angels of God's Love

SECTION TWO: PERSONAL MESSAGES FROM THE ANGELS

*P*eople Are Good?

I have talked to people about this over the years. Sometimes there are situations that just make it very difficult for you to see the good in an individual. It would be hard for me to tell someone that was beaten by another person, that the person doing the beating is a good person. It would be just as difficult for me to tell someone that had a family member murdered by someone, that the murderer is a good person. So I had to ask the Angels about this at the time of this writing. This is the answer I received about this concern.

February 23, 2009

"Our dearest Christine, we hear your words of concern on how to address these issues. We are here to tell you that no matter what someone does on earth, in our world, we see the good inside of each one of the people. We can tell you that there is a person inside that God made and crafted as finely as you were put into plan.

We will however instruct you with the fact that there is free will in your world. That is what will corrupt the humans faster than anything else. On the other hand we will tell you that God will not intervene with that free will because that is the promise He gave to the people, when the world was created.

We also know that your world put into action the plan that people will be corrected for their mistakes. This resembles the Universal Law that states if you do something that goes against what is written there will be a reaction to this situation. We tell you that with this rule there will be a reaction from this side of life to what happens on your side of life.

The plan was to have a world that would be loved by many. The plan was to have things in the world that would be cared for by many. The plan was for the people to have minds of their own to make their decisions in this way from the love of each other, from the love for God and all that was created for their use. The plan was for the humans to experience the growth of life.

So you can see now that sometimes the free will disrupts the plan. So lessons begin and lessons will be learned. Then we have the fact that people now need an opportunity to learn these lessons in a way they will be able to grow.

We also bestow upon each of you God's blessings. We will continue to send out the protection of God to each divine being on the earth plain. It is up to each person to choose to accept this offer and to live accordingly. As you have found, it is very hard to live this way because there are so many who have chosen to live in a disruptive manner to have control.

SECTION TWO: PERSONAL MESSAGES FROM THE ANGELS

Control is not all that it is measured either. Control is someone's free will to manipulate things to attract attention to them or to bring about a better life for themselves.

So you see there are many factors involved to free will and living a better life. There are many factors in just living this free life in your world. It is not hopeless and we in our kingdom have not given up on your world. We believe that God knows the perfect plan and will continue to supply for every need.

We have come forward to ask for the people of the world created by our God to reconsider your free will and live according to the God plan in action today. Follow the basics of life, live a life full of joy, watch for the positive in life and see it coming over and over again.

Please look at whatever your life is about today and make the necessary changes to bring about a balance and harmony. This is what is needed to live the life in the most precious manner, which life was meant to be.

Changes, many, many changes will occur and it is up to each individual to make the necessary changes in their own lives to correct the Universal imbalances of your world today.

Harmony is the reward. Harmony is the just desserts that many will receive for making any changes that can be made in the timely fashion.

Universal changes are needed today to allow your world to be functioning in the Harmony and Balance that is needed today.

> Your Angels of God's Love from Above

Celebration of Life

2005 Message:

"Happy Birthday! Yes today is your birthday. Every year we celebrate the day you came into the world and took your first breath of life. Each year on your special day is a celebration of your gift of life.

Each day you awaken refreshed and alive, so really each new morning is a Birth Day! Each day when you begin your day, celebrate a new day of life. Go out and find how you can celebrate.

Who will you ask to join in with you for this celebration? Where do you choose to go in your day? What do you chose to do with your new day? It is your chance at a new life of peace and well being in each day when you begin anew."

SECTION TWO: PERSONAL MESSAGES FROM THE ANGELS

*L*ooking Through God's Eyes

I have been asked by the Angels to see things and people through God's eyes and have told this to others. Someone once told me that they would not dare do that because they were not worthy of such an honor and it was sacrilegious. I asked about this and this is what I heard,

> "What a privilege it is to have the ability on a daily basis to see through God's eyes. It is not sacrilegious to do so! It is what is expected of you on a daily basis. It is when you do such a thing that you will experience a different view of your life as well as others.
>
> You will grow a great appreciation for life and for those around you. You will find you enjoy all of the things that are presented to you as Gifts from God in this lifetime. If you insist on keeping your eyes closed to all of this then your heart will never feel fulfilled. You will always feel a lack and you will always feel as if you are in the darkness of time.
>
> Open your eyes and see all of the beauty that is there for you to behold.
>
> Come little ones, open your eyes and view the world in the light that was meant for all to see.

We are waiting for you to partake in this wonderful gift of wisdom. Set yourselves free open the doors of opportunity to live, a life full of Love!"

What is Meditation?

Meditation is a means to transform or change the way the mind functions. It has been studied over the years and because of these studies it can now be called a science. It has been proven time and again that when used on a regular basis, it allows us to begin to experience the flow of the God Energy within our lives. It begins to bring about an Alignment of the Soul, it does lead us to be able to begin to identify with your whole being and the whole universe.

Meditation is safe and is very practical. It is a very simple way to balance a person's physical, spiritual, emotional and mental states of being. It will bring a balance to your whole system of living. It is what the Angels call, a Higher Form of Prayer to connect with the Divine Being of the God heart center.

SECTION TWO: PERSONAL MESSAGES FROM THE ANGELS

*W*hat is the Purpose of Meditation?

The main purpose of Meditation is to bring our conscious state of mind into a greater sense of awareness with the creator. It brings about a connection with the Divine source of all that is.

If we partner with that energy it will bring about a peace within and a growth beyond belief. Meditation is a very Spiritual experience and it becomes a divine prayer time.

The objective is to become aware of this Divine Energy of the God source. You will then be able to bring this energy within yourself. Allow this source to create an internal balance, bringing about a mental clarity and gradually grow into a higher spiritual being within this human body.

Meditation brings about a relaxed state of being within the mind, body and spirit. In return you will find that it brings about a sense of well-being. When you experience a state of well-being, you then bring about a much more balanced way of living into your path of life. This then allows for a more peaceful existence.

As I am typing these instructions on Meditation, I began to notice that the Angels are speaking here and they are helping me explain what I already know about meditation. They seem to want to take over here so I will have them give you their interpretations of this.

I will now turn this over to the Angels and have them explain what they want you to know about Meditation:

February 9, 2009

"The more you practice Meditation the more proficient you become with this exercise. In return for your practice, you will receive the knowledge, to begin to see a way to bring about a better way of living and an understanding of others in your world.

You will develop a higher Spiritual experience for your life. You will receive directions from God to bring about this better life. You will also be given instructions and receive the Wisdom of Understanding to know how to use these messages to begin to experience all of these things in your life.

There are those who receive higher teachings and are being asked to bring out these teachings to share with others. You can also receive these messages to help yourself through life and you will find that these instructions can be helpful to others."

This is what has happened to me over the years. I have found that these messages have helped others. That is why I finally decided to answer the Angel's request and put it in writing for the public to view.

The Angels continue the lesson on Meditation.

SECTION TWO: PERSONAL MESSAGES FROM THE ANGELS

*W*hy Should I Meditate?

"Meditation gives you what each of you craves, with all of your divine being. There is nothing else in this world that can bring about this feeling and bring to you what your heart desires as much as a strong meditation practice can.

Meditation hands you a mirror so you can see yourself like you have never been seen before. It opens the doors to all possibilities in the Universal way of life. It sets before your eyes a mirror for you to see yourself on the level that God sees you. It brings you clarity of mind and a peace that you will never experience in any other way. You will finally experience yourself on a different wave of energy than you could ever imagine could exist. You will begin to experience the true you, see the way of your path in this life and how to begin to accomplish things beyond your imagination.

Another name for Meditation is: The Path to the Soul

You can begin today to learn the process of staying attuned to this level of energy and become connected with the God force of all that is. You will begin to experience an accelerated level of energy within yourself that will lead you into many different arenas of life.

Enjoy the ride of the waves of the light! Take this journey with open eyes and an open mind. You will learn in an extremely higher vibratory rate.

This will lead to a new feeling of love for all beings and all creation. You will become more in tune with the Universal changes and will know intuitively what to do to adjust your level of energy in these situations.

The keys, to this process are: to begin your practice on a daily basis, put your whole heart and soul into each session and you will be rewarded accordingly. Your rewards will be Inner Peace and Transformation. Then you will have the ability to begin to send out this energy to the world. You will then find that you are able to make this energy a working force that has never been experienced before here in this world. This energy has the power of God, when used in the proper manner.

This is the same energy that Jesus used while He walked this earth plane only on a much higher level. It is a much higher level of consciousness, because there are groups of humans using it all at once. This is to accomplish what Jesus started so many years ago.

There are many Masters who have been called before. There are many Masters who are working behind the scenes now to help all those who are willing to work at this process on a regular basis.

Follow the instructions accordingly and find that you have the ability to help, to be the driving forces within the groups that are growing today as we speak to you.

These groups are growing stronger and stronger and we are ready to begin to utilize them in the very near future.

As you learn to stay attuned to this vital force within, you will experience an accelerated process of change and growth that leads to the maturing of love and fulfillment in your lives.

This is a very personal growth process and it takes practice. Do not give up and think you are doing it all wrong. Take it one step at a time and work with different types of Meditations until you find what works best for you.

Have fun with this process and do not work so hard on it. You will find that it flows much better that way. You will begin to grow and see things differently. You will also find that you are rewarded with a great sense of Inner Peace."

                The Angels of the Divine Source of the Light of God

The Angels have directed me to end this Section with the following message and meditation.

September 8, 2003

"Christine, Christine it is now time, to teach this lesson to others. Let the people know that each person is a part of our God. Because each person has this part we are all one, related in a way. These are the reasons we need to treat each other differently than you are treating one another at this time.

Great danger is lurking in your world due to the tremendous hatred being bred in people's hearts. It is time for each person to stop, become focused inside and then allow their hearts to melt. Once they warm their hearts to our God, their hearts will slowly start to warm to each other. This all takes time to happen, we understand that. Here is a meditation to teach. This will help the people go inside, to accomplish this for themselves."

Meditation #1: Melting Hatred with God's Love

"Begin by sitting comfortably and taking several cleansing breaths.

Breathe in through your nostrils and hold for a few seconds.

Blow out through your mouth with a force to make a noise as you release the breath. Do this at least three times releasing all the tension of the day.

Relax your whole body feeling the tension leaving from your feet.

Release your muscles in your skull, down through your face, relax your neck and shoulders, arms and hands.

Relax all of the muscles in your torso, feeling the tension releasing as it leaves down your thighs, past your knees, down through your calves and into your feet.

Feel yourself relax as the tension flows out, as your toes relax and all this tension energy flows out from the chakras of your feet. Leaving your body and mind in a state of relaxation and completely cleansed of all the negativity of your day.

Now begin to become aware of your heart as it beats. Listen to the sounds and follow the rhythm of the beats.

Feel this inside all throughout your body.

Remember the sensation of how your heart feels at this time in your body. Picture your heart now connecting with God's heart.

Begin to feel God's Love pouring into your heart. Open yourself up to the love, accept this love and feel it.

Now allow the love to travel out from your heart and go all through your body. The love now travels to your head, filling your mind to think love. It travels into your eyes, filling them with the ability to see love.

You can now see the love through God's eyes. Picture this, what do you see?

Now feel this sensation travel down your arms and into your hands, this gives you the ability to help others.

Start to practice sending out this love and peace to others. Send this to all of the different countries and into the world and all of the people, healing the world.

What do you feel with this sensation? You can now feel and see the love God has for all people, including you.

Sit for a few minutes and focus on this feeling and enjoy this new energy of Love, sent to you by God.

Gradually allow yourself to come back into the room and when you are ready open your eyes and become aware of your surrounding bringing with you the change that has occurred deep within yourself."

MEDITATION #1: MELTING HATRED WITH GOD'S LOVE

Write down any experiences you may have had in Meditation #1.

"Questions Answered By the Angels"

SECTION THREE

SECTION THREE: QUESTIONS ANSWERED BY THE ANGELS

WAITING

"My, my what a dear,

My, my we've all been waiting all this year.

What is there about this world,

that keeps us waiting just to hear?

Where is it all gone to this day in time?

What do you think with all on a dime?

Where do I go and what do I do?

We question and question all things through.

Finding the answer is what we request.

Finding an answer will give us great rest.

Seek in your hearts that joy which you seek.

This is where the answers lay,

you will find peace in less than a week."

Madrina *July 18, 2008*

SECTION THREE: QUESTIONS ANSWERED BY THE ANGELS

These are some of the questions that I have asked over the years and the answers that I have received from the Angels.

Are The Angels from God?

Many people over time ask me how I know where these Angels come from. They want to make sure that I am not speaking to the dark side. I felt I would add a section asking the Angels were they from God.

The Angels I talk with never discourage me from loving others or loving God. They always encourage me to move forward with my life and help where there is help needed. They have pointed me in directions over the years in my studies that have brought people into my life that need to know they are not alone.

A lady once told me that the Angels were not real and not from God. She said that books written about the Angels or Angel communication never mentioned God.

She believed that this could not be real. She told me that we are not to worship the Angels. I said to her that I do not worship Angels I talk to them, just as I talk to a friend. I am here to tell you that the Angels have never taken credit for anything without the power of God directing them.

I ended up asking the Angels to send me an answer to this topic. This is what they say about it:

> "We are God's messengers and God's Helpers. We are here working amongst you now to bring the Love of God to each and every person. We also say that without God we would not exist and would not be able to be with all of you."

On this same topic I had received this message on

September 9, 1996,

> "Dear Christine,
>
> "My sweet, I am always with you. I am from God with Love.
>
> Without God, I can not be, as well as you can not be! I am sent by God as His Messenger to guide you spiritually, morally, mentally and physically."
>
>
> Your Angels of God's Light and Love

SECTION THREE: QUESTIONS ANSWERED BY THE ANGELS

I did do some research of my own to find out how many times there were Angel encounters or happenings in the Bible and this is what I found. In the Old Testament, Angels were mentioned 117 times in 108 verses. In the New Testament they were mentioned 182 times in 172 verses.

What people say about communicating with the Angels really does not matter to me anymore. I know with no doubt that these messages are from a higher source. They refer to themselves as Angels. My first written message was signed from the Angel of God's Love. They instantly give credit to God all the time.

*C*an anyone talk to the Angels?

Someone once told me they did not believe they could hear God or the Angels. I told them what the Angels told me.

> "Listen to the wind in the trees, feel the warmth of the sun on your face, hear the whisper of the waves of the ocean. How do you feel when someone you love hugs you?
>
> The voice of God or the touch of an Angel is in each of these experiences and many more. God does not walk that far from any of us."
>
> I do not know a vengeful God. I only know a loving God!

It is what mankind does with their lives that make things wrong in the world."

The Angels of God's Light

With this entry from the Angels, I have to say YES, everyone has experiences with the Angels. Anyone can have their Angel work in their life. All you need to do is ask. I am told that we have free will and they can not intervene in our life unless we first invite them in. So begin today asking for your Angels' help in your life then sit back and pay attention to what happens around you. You will become more aware of your surroundings, you will start to notice changes within yourself and how you look at life and other people.

New Testament in Luke 1:19: <u>New American Standard Bible (©1995)</u> The angel answered and said to him, *"I am Gabriel, who stands in the presence of God, and I have been sent to speak to you and to bring you this good news.*

How many Angels are there?

Over the years people have asked me many questions about the Angels. One of the questions was at a seminar that I was giving a talk about "Talking with the Angels". I was asked by one of the ladies, "How many Angels are there?" I told her it depended on what book you read.

SECTION THREE: QUESTIONS ANSWERED BY THE ANGELS

I was only joking with her but I do not think people there understood that. I then told them that I was not an expert on the history of Angels I was only asked to teach people how to talk and work with them. That is what the Angels asked me to do.

On my way home that night one of my Angels said to me,

"That was not a very good answer, Christine. In the future, if someone asks you that question again, here is what you should tell him or her.

"There are as many Angels as there are people in this world. There are as many Angels as there are problems or situations in life. There is an Angel for everything that exists in this world."

I thought to myself, man that is a lot of Angels! Think about that for just a minute and see what you can picture in your head! I can see a whole big crowd of Angels!

I looked up to see if there were any references on how many Angels were in the bible. Several references were made about this and here is one: **Dan 7:10** *"A fiery stream issued and came forth from before him: thousand thousands ministered unto him, and ten thousand times ten thousand stood before him: the judgment was set, and the books were opened."*

ANGEL TALK / CHATTING WITH THE ANGELS

*T*he Angels Answer Friends Questions

As I was writing this book the Angels asked me to send out a request to my friends. They asked for them to send me their questions and we would do our best to answer them. Some of the questions I did not include in this book because they were personal.

I did include the Angels answers in other cases, because they answered them in a way that if someone else needed this help it would give them some peace and answers also. They always tell me that there normally can be more than one person going through some of the same things at the same time in life or at least have had similar experiences.

These people are very dear friends of mine and I wish them the best in their lives. I would like to let each of them know, how much I appreciate them for allowing me the privilege of using their questions and the Angels answers in this book. I have however kept their names out of the questions and answers to protect their privacy.

Here are some messages that have become wonderful answers from the Angels.

The first message will convey some instructions about a situation that many people are going through in their lives, at the time of writing this book.

SECTION THREE: QUESTIONS ANSWERED BY THE ANGELS

I found this very interesting and have been working with these ideas since. I have found them to be very powerful in my life and have seen changes occurring because of it all.

For anyone who is dealing with hardships over money or loss of income and feeling a little bit lost, this is a great message for you from the Angels.

One of the things the Angels have always impressed upon me is that they can never tell us every step of the way what to do or not to do. They can only make some requests or give us advice on some ideas to try. They make a comment about this issue in this response.

Direction in Life and Financial Guidance

This question asked about a direction in life and some financial situations. I am asking the Angels your personal question for you. This is the reply that I am receiving as I type back to you.

"Our sweet Angel of Light! This is a real dilemma that you are facing at this time in your life. We must tell you we are not in a position in our role in your life to tell you how to run your life. We can give you some insight as to what the problems may be and some suggestions on how to make life a bit better for you and your family.

It seems that you are faced with cutting back extremely on spending at this time. You are being shown an easier and less stressful way of living. When you require less you can make less money and still have plenty to go around in life. We see the ability for you to stretch your dollars to cover more than you can see at this time.

We would like to encourage you, to move forward with the beautiful work that you are doing.

If this is not a possibility at his time then we understand that. There is a possibility of a second place to work that will be coming your way soon. Pay close attention to this possibility, this opportunity. This takes much time to build and become prosperous in this work.

Many times our prosperity is slow in coming because of our blocks with the flow of money in our minds, other times the block is a physical obstruction with money.

In your case you are blocking your flow with a physical symptom of the desire to have more money. If you can let go of that desire and see that more money is there already. See this with your heart, mind and spirit. Then let go of all that is needed and believe that need is already fulfilled. This will help the flow come to you more quickly.

The world right now is practicing from a lack of things. Everything is creeping up in cost and it is because of all of the talk of recession and lack of things in people's lives.

SECTION THREE: QUESTIONS ANSWERED BY THE ANGELS

People are losing jobs according to their thoughts; they are losing homes, money and other things.

Think instead of what you are gaining, opportunity, opportunities and many opportunities. Instead say, I am gaining a new possibility to do something I want to do now with this job out of my life, the door opens to all new things to come!

Loss of the house, I am now ready to move forward without the anchor of responsibility of a house to maintain.

Loss of money is always so much harder to explain to humans. It is not a loss of money even though it seems that way. The money not coming is a matter of refocusing on money as something we do not need any more.

We only have a need to function in this world. What does it take to function here? We need a place to live, something to eat and a way to get around, happiness and contentment.

When we put our needs out there in a physical way, instead of a lack of money, it is not coming or I can not afford it because I do not have the money to get it, then we will see things coming to us over and over again.

Start with a plan our dear, start with a simple plan of what you will need in your life to live a great and wonderful life. Make it very simple to start with, and then let it grow from there!

Map it out make it with pictures and words if you need to. That will keep it fresh in your mind over and over again. Then make a conscious decision where you want to be and what you really want to do. Write that goal down.

The next step is to make a time frame and let go of time and how is it going to happen. It is hard to just let go of the how to in life.

How do I make it happen is always a question people ask us. You do not make it happen, you allow it into your life and allow it to happen.

Make space in your life for it to flow to you. Do not clutter up your space and time so much that there is no more room for it to come to you. Then daily or hourly whatever works best for you, decide that you are happy with the outcome of each day. You are happy no matter what happens because it is an opportunity to grow and an opportunity for adventure in your life.

Plan on being happy, prosperous and make no room for anything else but that. Whatever means it takes to have these two things happen in your life, you should then take that road at this time.

It is only about what works best in your life to bring about a peace and contentment in your life, right now.

SECTION THREE: QUESTIONS ANSWERED BY THE ANGELS

We wish you all the happiness, the joy and excitement in your life that you have exuded out to others. It will all come back to you our dearest.

You must take this into your hands and make it work. Do not sit back and wait for things to come your way. Take the bull by the horns and bring about the change that you so deserve.

We know that we have not told you to quit doing one thing and do another.

We have not told you that you need to get rid of the trouble of money from your life. We have given you a map to follow to help you move past this time in a more peaceful way, whichever way you decide to move in your life.

Hopefully this will help you find a direction for your life. Put the process to work for at least ninety days and then see if you begin to see a difference in your life.

Love and the Light of God are sent to you. A Healing is coming over you as we sing a song of Joy just for you! Celebration, Celebration, Celebration sent your way!"

Your Angels of the Light

The Angels say with this message they know that so many others are bothered by the same questions in life.

It is their hope that this message will help so many others be able to look at the money situations in their life in a different way.

If you can, they say that it will make a major difference in the way the world situations affects their lives.

Finding Direction and Answers in Life

The next question is one that many seem to want to know and it is a very good question to ask your Angels to find some direction or to find an answer for situations happening at this time in life.

My question is: What is it that I need to know at this time in my life?

> "You are our dearest, sweetest child of God. So curious about life and so full of living! What a wonderful ride you have had. We know that there has been much trouble in your life we can see that. You still shine so brightly through it all and you just keep the faith so well. We see your light and we see your curiosity.

SECTION THREE: QUESTIONS ANSWERED BY THE ANGELS

We also see that you sometimes do not believe what we have just told you about yourself. So tonight we will ask you to work on your self-confidence and your self-acceptance of you.

We want you to look into the mirror and tell yourself that you are loved. God is so good and has made you this way to accomplish the things in life you will need to accomplish.

You then ask us what you need to accomplish. You are to try to remember where you came from my dear child! Where did I come from you now ask, well you came from our side. You came from our heart. You came from our creator's love. What could be wrong with that?

We want you to know right now at this very moment that you are loved. You have not felt that for a while we hear. We are here to tell you, that you just have not been able to look around because of your blinders that you wear.

You have successfully blocked out the things you can not understand and live in a blur. That blur keeps you from progressing. With these feelings you can not move forward with your work, studies or your life.

We ask you now to physically feel these blinders, really take your hands, lift them off your face and throw them away, you no long need them. Once this happens plan on seeing things in a different light!

Know that we are here to help you to accomplish this. Once you have done that and left those blinders behind, you will know we are here for you again. We have always been here but now you will know it.

We will begin again to shine the light on the path that is laid before you, the path of a spiritual growth that will blossom into a beautiful rose!

We want you to know we are assigned to you to help you grow. To help you fly free of all self - doubt and self prison that you have put yourself in. The bars are removed from the cage and you are now free to step out and smell the roses in life!

Enjoy the beauty and the scent of life now that you are free to begin living again. It is plain and simple dear one plain and simple. Enjoy the beauty that is all around you every day!

We are allowing you to now live in that beauty because it is your right to do so! Claim your rights, stand up and shout that you will claim victory over all that has repressed you over that time. Now you stand on top of the hill as Queen of that hill. Victory is yours dear one! Victory is yours"

Love is sent to you from your Angel of Self - Love and Peace

The Angels want everyone to know that you no longer need to be blinded by self -doubt and fear.

SECTION THREE: QUESTIONS ANSWERED BY THE ANGELS

They want you to understand, you just need to remember you have the help you need to break free from the things in life that are stopping you from moving forward with your life. Take a hold of your life and claim your Victory!

Learning to Listen and Finding your Spiritual Path

This wonderful woman has asked a great question because so many of us get frustrated when we think we are not moving forward with our growth. The Angels will give you their opinions on how they interpret where we are on our spiritual growth at this time.

Once on this spiritual quest we do seem to find so much we want to learn and we all want it right now. We either try way too hard or we take on way too many studies so that we bog ourselves down to the point that we can not move forward. This is because it is just too hard to pick up the load and carry it. So here is the answer from the Angels for this.

PLEASE, PLEASE, PLEASE, include me with my personal question. I feel like I am stuck spiritually. I want to learn to listen to my angels and hear my messages, to become a medium. I read everything I can get my hands on and take every class that is offered, but why can I not progress??? Thank you my friend.

This is what I hear from an Angel that flies in when I read your question:

My dearest sweet little one,

"We want to impress upon you at this time that if you want something to happen in this work it is now time to focus in on just one thing at a time. What do you want to learn the most in this spiritual work? Make a decision on what you want to learn then proceed from there. Once you make your mind up to learn that topic then take just that one thing and find a way to learn it.

Talking to the Angels is very simple really, you just talk to us in the same way you would talk with anyone. Then you must learn to listen. That will be the hardest thing to do for most because you do not believe you can. So we must move past the thing that stops most people and that is self-doubt.

Start with something very small and ask for confirmation on the answer. Then see what you get on it. Look for clues and look for things to come into your mind or things to come into your life with the answer. Sometimes it comes in the form of someone you are talking with just mentioning it to you and you will understand from what they say.

There are so many ways we can work from the Angelic realm to get the answers to you.

SECTION THREE: QUESTIONS ANSWERED BY THE ANGELS

Now as for your growth per say, you are growing every day. We see that from our perspective.

Do not ever think that you are not moving forward. As humans you always think you are standing still but you really are not.

Right now you are cultivating what you have planted. You are feeding your spirituality, so go ahead and feed away. You will one day just sit up in bed and say Wow is that all there is to it? It will just happen out of the blue for you. So hang in there, you are doing your best with what you have to learn from.

Remember now to just take one thing to find your focus and that is what you will want to put your attention to doing. Our little beautiful lady we say, just take one step at a time toward your goals. You will find the way to what you desire the most."

Your Angel of God's Love and Light

This is the response to this message: You have no idea how much your message means to me, and BAMMMM, you hit the nail right on the head! I am asking for help to get me more self-confidence, I have always known that is my weakest point.

Thank you Sweet Christine. I hope to see you soon!

Thank you, you answered my heart desire! Thank you.

*L*iving to be pleasing to God

This next question I am told that we really are way too hard on ourselves. We expect far more from ourselves than God would ever expect. What God wished for each of us is, for us to be happy with life and appreciate all that is given to us in this lifetime.

Here is the next question and answer from the Angels. There are so many people who tell me that they are having trouble believing they are living up to what they think they need to do to please God.

I am asking the Angels for an answer tonight to this question. This is what I heard:

Our dearest child,

"You will never be a disappointment to our God! You are way too hard on yourself. God already made you perfect. All you need to do is love God with all of your heart, mind and soul. Then treat your fellow person with love, dignity and respect.

Humans only fall short on what God wants in their mind. God will always love his family no matter what you do.

You only need to talk with God when you do something you know you just slipped up on. Tell God what is bothering you and what you might have done, no matter what happened.

SECTION THREE: QUESTIONS ANSWERED BY THE ANGELS

God will work with you to help you let go of what bothers you about it all. Once you know you have done something that bothers you and you have told God you are sorry, it is over in God's world. If you must make amends in your world then you will be able to do so knowing that all is well with God.

Carry God in your heart and you will always be lead in a divine direction. Know that the light will always be on in God's heart where you are concerned. We are all a part of God and so we have a natural knowing of what is right living and what is not. So pay attention to that little voice that speaks inside yourself and know we are leading you in the direction that will one day lead you home to God.

Never question if you have a place on our side of life, it is here and we will help you along the way.

Your time on earth is to be fun and exciting. Find your fun at every corner and see the adventure that awaits you along the way. Laugh and smile at things that would normally bother you. You will find much more humor in life and it will treat you to a happy day!

It is our wish to be a guiding force in your life and to help you as we can."

Your loving Angels of Joy!

Goal to be ordained

This message is for someone special to me who asked about her goal to be ordained and if that will happen for her.

"Our light and shining angel! We want to speak today about your goals that you are asking to accomplish.

Ordination and family tree both take a lot of time to accomplish, time you do not have at this time in your life. You are devoting yourself to your family and doing what is needed there first.

That is what needs to be happening right now. You are accomplishing much with the time you have with your family.

When it comes time to take care of you, this is put on the back burner per say. When people do that to themselves, it is putting their lives on hold.

Until you take your life off hold and put it back into action things will not get accomplished for you very quickly.

Busy, Busy, Busy for others, brings about an imbalance in your life for you. This is focused on just one sideof things in life. That is the helping others all the time over what you want. There is nothing at all wrong with this situation.

SECTION THREE: QUESTIONS ANSWERED BY THE ANGELS

We thank you for all that you have done and continue to do for others. BUT on the same token you are neglecting yourself.

Please find a balance in what you want to accomplish for yourself and what others seek you to do for them. Then you will find that you can accomplish what is in your hearts desire as soon as you desire to do so.

If becoming ordained is your dream, then make it happen. Only you can do just that by not allowing things to get in the way.

No more excuses our dear one. No more reasons why someone or something stopped you. They really are not excuses but you must let this type of thing not get in your way.

If there is a person causing this situation to not happen, then find someone else who will accomplish this with you. Find other ways to accomplish what you are seeking.

We feel the family tree is very overwhelming for you right now. When it becomes fun for you again and not a struggle, then the energy will come back again. Once that happens you can tackle what you need to finish this project. But a finished project we do show you in the end.

For the items or information you can not get, you will just need to move past that at this time. Do what you can it will be very interesting how close you will become with some of the family once they find each other over time.

Continue to strive to do good for others in your lifetime. You will accomplish much in that area of your life. You are an Earth Angel and are helping many in their path in life. So keep the torch lit for others to see! Know you will light the world a blaze for God and to find their Spiritual light within themselves.

Blessing sweet child of God, Blessings. Know that what you put your mind to in a solid way, WILL become reality."

Your Angels of God's Accomplishments and wisdom

The Angels tell us that when we make our lives so busy with doing things or we have too much clutter around us, we do not make room for other things to be accomplished.

So if you see that something is not happening for you, but you know this is what you feel you want, make a quick check up in your life. Then see where you are working too hard at something or having too much conflict within the space you are in.

SECTION THREE: QUESTIONS ANSWERED BY THE ANGELS

Look at what you need to change or get rid of in your life. What clutter is stopping you from moving forward. If once you have reassessed your life and what you have asked for has still not happened, then know that God knows what is best, for you at this time. Trust that God knew whatever it is was not right at this time for your life.

A Change of Employment & Spiritual Growth

This next question deals with a person who is looking at a change of employment and asks for advice on this matter. She is also growing spiritually and asked some questions about the spiritual growth.

Our sweet child of God,

"You are a wonder of the light and love of God, we just enjoy watching you as you touch more and more lives. You are amazing at how you work towards helping others. As for your life and being just plain tired of the way it is, we will do what we can to answer you in the best way we can at this time.

It is our belief that you will have to make this decision on which job location to be in. What we can do for you though is this. We can be there for you with gentle nudges along the way.

Things begin to happen and before you know it you will be doing what you need to do in life and wonder how it ever happened this way. That is how you know we worked for your best interest.

We do ask you to stop in your day and start to feel again. Feel what is inside yourself and see what you have been doing with things lately.

Stop and take time to ask yourself what holds you where you are, freedom, job security, or is it what you know? Are you afraid to take on something new?

We tell you once you do the tallying on this decision you will know which is the right way to go for you. Ask and we will present you with information about both places. You will know by this information that you find out about which place you would rather be working at.

There are all kinds of jobs, do them the best you know how to do and plan to make advancements.

You are on a growth cycle right now and you will need this experience with this growth to help you grow stronger in your next life cycle.

Plan on growing stronger within the structure you are in at this time.

SECTION THREE: QUESTIONS ANSWERED BY THE ANGELS

Then plan on excelling past this structure in a short period of time. Know that there will be changes in the location you are in at this time in life.

This will help you make your decision and feel secure in this decision. Once you have made up your mind, you will be able to look back on it with pride because of how you are carrying yourself with this job you are in now."

Blessing sweet child, Blessing,

Angels of the blessed

What makes you comfortable and The Selling of a house.

I am working on some answers for you from the Angels and hopefully something will make some sense for you. This friend has a situation where she is trying to decide if what she is involved with is something she still should be doing.

Dearest child,

"This question makes you uncomfortable. You do not want to hurt a friend by not doing things the same as they do.

That is a very nice thing, but if you are uncomfortable with this situation then you just can not do it.

It will not work unless you are more comfortable with the process. You should not do something that you are not comfortable with.

We see you are really more uncomfortable bothering people. This situation is understandable, so if it causes you stress then it is not something that you need to do. If this would come naturally then it is something you can pursue."

Will my house sell? When? Is there something I should be doing to help it sell?

"If you really want your house to sell then it will. We do not see it at this time for a bit. We see you staying on for a bit longer if you want to make the money on the house. You could sell your house for less money and it would sell. If you want to make bigger money, it is advisable to wait out the process for the right person with the big bucks to be ready to buy. We do see you can afford to stay and it really is not inconvenient for you to stay so it seems that the energy will keep you there for the time being.

If you truly want the house to sell sooner, then it would be time to make the energy better in the house. It is close in the house the energy is not flowing properly for the sale of the house.

SECTION THREE: QUESTIONS ANSWERED BY THE ANGELS

You will need to do the releasing, some energy balancing of the house. Talk to the guides to find the person and prepare them to come right away to look to work something out with you.

As we say the timing is not right and the person is not ready just yet that will really need the property in that area. Start putting it out in the Universe, the person purchasing the property for the said amount is ready to move forward with their lives and that will include the purchase of the house."

*P*ersonal Journey

Is there something I should be working on (development or a hobby or something else) that I am not?

"Your growth is a very personal journey and things often get in the way. You will need to re-visualize things for your life and then you will start to move forward.

Work on learning more about your Spiritual quest.

You do read, but sometimes you will need to write while reading, so that you have a journal at the end of the book of words that you forgot were there.

We are asking you to find one thing that will help your Spiritual journey grow.

It is possible that the healing will be something you will want to learn and then share with someone else. Continue to work on learning more about the healing work the best you can."

Spiritual Path and Help for a Loved One

Where is my Spiritual path headed? Do you see the person I asked you about getting help for his problem?

Our brilliant light and loving Angel,

> "Your path is growing all the time with your spirituality. It is only when you allow yourself to become so tired that you feel that you are not growing. Your path is being used on a daily basis. Some people are called to walk out in the world and help others grow daily. Others are called to be used on a daily basis and touch the people's lives that they come in contact with each day. You do just that.
>
> You are always on the look out for others to help. You always put others first in what you do in life.
>
> You will always have our love and warm hugs little one! We fondly look upon you in the evenings when you do your prayers. We know you are doing the best you can each and every day. Your path is your life's journey and you touch others in a way that most do not understand. You affect people's lives and you may never really know in what way.

SECTION THREE: QUESTIONS ANSWERED BY THE ANGELS

That is okay, because you do not need to know each time you touch someone. It is just so natural and it comes from your heart every time. You stop throughout your day because someone will just come by where you are. You take the time needed to listen and offer a kind word.

So you might not think kindness all the time at work, but sometimes life can get a bit trying. That is when you will need to take a step back, re-evaluate the situation and see if you reacted accordingly. You must stand up for yourself and take care of yourself, that way you will have the energy to keep going in life.

We take you for Angel rides at night while you sleep and we refresh you for your new days. We will continue to work with you always. We will not allow you to fall and we will carry you when you need us to.

By now you do not even need to ask, we will see it when you need it and be there instantly!

Your awards await you and we will see to it that you have many rewards during your lifetime.

Your grandchildren are a blessing and will continue to grow healthy and strong. Another will come along in a little while. The light is on, burning bright and waiting for just the right moment to spring the surprise."

Now for your next question: (I have changed the name and make reference to Pat-him/he, to protect the person that was asked about).

> "What a gift even though sometimes people are not sure. This person is such a loving soul and a good-natured person. Pat shines here for you. He is hard driven and works hard. Look at this person's inner love for you and look at the great love for family. Pat has a deep down drive to move forward in this life. We can help this person with the needs, but first, he will need to ask for this help.
>
> We cannot intervene for people because of free will, so he can ask for a special healing and we will work with that request.
>
> Take the love and all that this person has to give you. Love Pat in return, which comes easy for you because your heart is filled with love!
>
> Tell him that we will keep this world safe and God loves him. The Angels look out for this person every day because of the love in the heart, the kindness and gentleness that is shown for others. Know that all will be taken care of with you both.
>
> It is time to fly now, so hold on tight and get ready to fly with us again and again.

SECTION THREE: QUESTIONS ANSWERED BY THE ANGELS

See the lights shining so bright see the light shine to lead the way. Shine so brightly shine so brightly let the light shine the way."

Your Angels of Divine Guidance.

Career and Personal Goals

My question is about guidance and what I need to be most concerned with at this time, including career and personal goals.

Our beloved,

"We must come to you tonight with our love for your kindness to others. We must recognize you for your efforts in life. We tell you that we appreciate you for your energy that you give to others. Your smile is contagious.

Now we will give you some guidance tonight our dear child of God. We will try to direct you with what is most important for you at this time.

Career we hear changes, many, many changes coming approaching quickly. Look to the future with your career. Make your decisions on what work is to you. This place you are in now will continue for you but you must stand clear and allow what is to happen, happen and not get in the way. Do your job and keep yourself away from those who are not.

Continue on your spiritual journey and your learning. Continue on your healing journey and your spirit works. Keep letting us inspire you with the works of your hands. Continue to create the wonderful things you can create. They will keep magnifying as you do more work with your hands. Your visions will become clearer in a faster way. You are beginning to see more of what you are asked to do with these creations. There will be more to do, so watch and listen to what we ask of you. Create, Create and continue to Create. Each piece has a special Angel blessing from us. So focus as you make these pieces and know we have a hand in it all.

Create a plan for yourself when it comes to your personal life and your spiritual directions.

Begin today to know what it is you are searching for, write it down and create it just as you create your wonderful gifts. Know when you put your mind to something it will become a reality.

Remember when you are feeling a bit down we are here helping you continue to fly. Call on us for a wonderful ride to the clouds with us. We will take you beyond your wildest dreams. Float away with us our wonderful young man, float away with us to your dreams and your reality. Allow us to take you away on a daily basis. You will begin to see your path and your journey. Know that your path has been traveled well by you to this point.

SECTION THREE: QUESTIONS ANSWERED BY THE ANGELS

Know that all is in divine order and you are learning as you go. We will continue to bless you and keep you in our care.

The glorious band of light will surround you always, know that our light will always shine for you to see and you will never be alone as long as you fly with us into eternity!

Always keep your head up and your smile on. Our light will always shine through and help those who need it.

Praise the God in the heavens and beyond, know that the God spark is eternal in your heart and soul!"

Your Angels of God's Blessed Love and Divine Spark of Life

About Your Job

Our dearest sweet child,

"You are our sunshine child. The sun shines on you from above to bring about happiness to your life. The road you have traveled has been a bumpy one to say the least. We are showing you a way to walk a smoother life. The road ahead will not weave to and fro any longer. We have smoothed the trail. You can help with this by stopping in your daily life, take a deep breath and relax into our arms of safety. We will catch you every time.

Listen closely to us dear child and we will whisper the words of comfort for you. Love and joy will come to you.

As for your question about your job, we ask you to look through different eyes than you see through at this time. We ask that you find a way to see opportunity in all that you are up against. We will have you look differently at this situation you are in.

We would like for you to break the situations down into small pieces so you do not get so overwhelmed and look at it in a positive way to see the positive changes this could bring to your life.

The education you seek will only be short term. It will end in a wonderful experience and opportunity for you to grow in a field you find interesting. You will be able to work through the education process in which you stated. It would be less income.

We will tell you this differently. As a nurses aid, you have the opportunity to be making more money because you still have your settlement money in addition to the extra money you will be making as a nurses aid.

We encourage you to look to the future and then see where you want to be in five years. Do you want to be in a job that seems to bring you grief or do you want to change your future to bring about inner peace?

SECTION THREE: QUESTIONS ANSWERED BY THE ANGELS

Now we tell you that you can also change the way you react to things at your present job so you can handle it differently and stay there. What opportunities do you have in your present environment? Are there more opportunities in your future going forward with what you are going to school for?

Will you stay with the present company after you graduate from school? If not, then time could be at the present to except money and benefits while you are getting on your feet, to move forward towards your goals.

You see we are giving you options to choose from. We are trying to lay things out in a clearer picture for you so you can see things differently and clearly. Make up your mind and move forward with your life. If you stay stagnant and dormant you will not grow.

You must make your mind up to move forward in some way. Be it for a change in the way you look at your present job, go to school and adjust your emotions or change the work you do with some other company and school. That will be your choice in the long run.

We are here to support you along the way and help you see the light ahead more brightly. Whatever your decision is, we will be right beside you along the way.

Pay attention to your inner person when you put the options listed above down on paper and read them back to yourself.

If you feel tension with either then find a way to change that tension to bring about a balance. Bring back your inner peace about your life.

Meditate on the outcome to be positive no matter what you decide and move forward on that note. Put your best foot forward and see it for the best outcome for you and your life. That way when you look back at this, you will see that you are making the best choice, for this time in your life.

Life might feel overwhelming at times for you our dear. Remember to take some deep breaths and keep a positive attitude each day about the experiences you have. You will get your answers with a peace inside that you can live on forever.

We do see you working in a field that is helping others. Your hands are your gift, to be giving to others in a healing environment. So anyway you get there is up to you. We see you as a wonderful healing energy that will be in the field of helping others.

This is what we have to give you at this time. Shine your light to the world and all will see your inner beauty dear one."

Shine on,   Your Angels of Peace and Harmony

Thank you so much for the beautiful message from the angels, Christine! I feel much better about these developments now :)

SECTION THREE: QUESTIONS ANSWERED BY THE ANGELS

*C*ontentment and Peace of Mind

Dear Angels, "What changes must I make to bring contentment and peace of mind back into my life?" What do you have to say tonight about this?

> "You are a sweet soul and child of God. Do not be so hard on yourself. You are such a blessing to so many. You tend to tire yourself out with the worry of others.
>
> Sometimes things and situations are put into other people's lives to help them grow. Worry does not help these situations.
>
> Offer up a prayer for those you can do nothing to help. Prayer is a guiding light for others to begin to see their way in life.
>
> Change is not an easy thing for people to experience. Change sometimes is necessary to bring the new energy to light. Sometimes it is a change only in our attitude, which will bring about the healing that is needed.
>
> With you our dearest we tell you not to worry. Put the worry into the light of God's heart and allow this wonderful energy to heal the situation.
>
> Claim your happiness and settle for no less! Claim your rewards and expect them!

We can only tell you that life is a struggle sometimes but it is in the battle that we build ourselves by fighting the energy that is flowing in. This brings about conflict in our lives. If we can sit back and just allow things to unfold, we have less conflict in our lives. This is not always so easy because human nature wants to fix everything. Sometimes things will not be fixed without conflict.

So when you begin to feel this overwhelming feeling that just overcomes you and brings you down, stop, look around, then begin listening to what is happening and see the results.

If the result is conflict, anger, resentment, bitterness and/or unhappiness, then know that there is an imbalance. Find out what needs to be let go of to bring about peace. Sometimes it is as easy as control.

Do not take on the baggage that is too heavy to carry. Allow God to carry this burden.

That is what this promise is about. God will carry all of your burdens that are too heavy and do not seem to have answers at this time.

Sometimes situations need to brew a bit before there is an answer. Other times the answers come right away. The brewing takes time before it is done and things can change.

SECTION THREE: QUESTIONS ANSWERED BY THE ANGELS

This is the time when you will feel the conflict, when you resist the time of brewing. Allow things to simmer and do not try to turn the heat down.

Take a step back and watch as things unfold and take on the time of rest. When you just can not do anything to change the way things are going, give up and rest a bit. After a little while you will see that things went according to God's divine plan.

Do not resist things, do not fight it anymore allow it and allow God in to carry some of the load. Take a deep breath and turn over your burdens for others to carry on their own.

If someone is not happy with something, you can be there as a support. You can carry a positive energy toward this and allow the situation to unfold.

When you choose happiness in your day then happiness follows every time. When you choose chaos and strife, then it will find you also. So remember to smile deeply and allow yourself to rest when time is calling for rest. React and move forward when times are calling for you to do this. Let go and allow God when things are out of your control. God is the greatest conductor and knows the road to success for all things.

We send our blessings of happiness and healing of your past life strife's.

We know you have had a lot of strife in your life. The burdens can be heavy at times but allow us to help. We can fly you off for an adventure whenever you ask. We can carry you to the highest point of relaxation if you ask us to. So allow us in and allow us to work with you and we will be there without fail.

Peace to you our dearest child, peace, contentment and healing."

Your Angels of Divine Happiness and Joy

How do you learn to talk to your Angel?

So you might be thinking about now, "How on earth do I get to talk to my Angel?" Well, this is where we will help you learn how to do just that.

2nd Assignment: Talking With your Angels:

"* **First** of all you have to **believe** or at the very least have a feeling that maybe you can! That is most important. Some people really did not believe they could and they have had an experience that helped them awaken to the fact that there really are Angels. Then again other times we need to take time out of our lives to stop and just ask them to be there.

* This is the **Second** thing that needs to happen, you will only need to **ask**. Then Angels say that we are waiting for you to ask.

*Believe and now Ask! How do I do that you might want to know? All you have to do is put into words or your thoughts something like this.

Angels, will you work with me? Or Angels are you there? Or Angels, can you talk to me?

ANGEL TALK / CHATTING WITH THE ANGELS

Do you understand now? All you really need to do is ask in whatever way it works for you and in your own words because this is personal and it is for you.

Third step is to *listen*! Once you have asked for your Angels to come into your life and make them known, then just listen.

*Believe, Ask and now Listen.

Do not just believe that it is only your imagination or that you can not hear a thing! If you say I did not get anything, I never get anything so this does not work or this is not real, you block yourself from your experience.

***Fourth step:** Tell yourself that you do have something and find it. Look for it and it will be there. Even if it is the smallest of lights, or just a few words, or just a very small piece of glitter you do have something magnificent!

***Fifth step**: *Write* down what it is that you experienced once you have asked.

If you really did not feel, see or hear anything push yourself a little harder. Stop a minute and write down the very first thought, picture, feeling or emotion that you experienced.

That will be your very first Angel Message! This allows you to trust that you really did get something.

2ND ASSIGNMENT: TALKING WITH YOUR ANGELS

Believe, Ask, Listen, You have it, Write it down and now Trust.

***Sixth step:** *Trust* that you have your Angel walking or flying right beside you.

Believe, Ask, Listen, Write it down, Trust and now most importantly and we know you have heard this over and over again, but be Grateful!

***Seventh step:** *Gratitude* will take you many places and will fill you with so much love and peace. Gratitude is the greatest healer for anything going on in your life.

When you are grateful for things in your life you begin to see all of the gifts from God. You will find you need less and less in your life that have no meaning. You will be drawn to people, things and places that you do not understand why but know that it is right. So live with a grateful heart and you will do well by it.

Now we have determined that you need to:
Remember to Believe, Ask, Listen, You have it, Write it Down, Trust and be Grateful, that is really all there is to finding your Angel in your life. Get ready for new doors to open. Expect a wonderful adventure, when you begin your new life. as you begin to take your flight with the Angels."

Write down your first Angel Message here:

2ND ASSIGNMENT: TALKING WITH YOUR ANGELS

*M*editation #2: *Meeting your Personal Angel*

Allow about 15 – 20 minutes for this meditation.

"This is a Guided Meditation but if you find that you are being guided to go in a different direction let your time be yours and go where you are being guided. This guidance is only for those who prefer to have a visual meditation.

I. Read through the first paragraph and then put the book down.

a. Take time now to stop reading and just focus inside yourself only for a moment and feel who you are! Listen now to that little voice inside, pay attention to all those sent to help you. God has sent guides, to help guide you, Angels, to inspire and heal you, and then your loved ones, to let you know they are here to help you and bring you their love!

II. It is now time to start this Meditation with a deep breath being taken in through your nostrils to the count of 8, hold it to the count of 8 and then slowly release the breath through your mouth, to the count of 8 and hold the time before you inhale again to the count of 8. (Do this to your comfort level on the count).

MEDITATION #2: MEETING YOUR PERSONAL ANGEL

We will take you on a flight with the Angels in this meditation:

Close your eyes and allow your breathing to become shallow.

Your breath comes slower and easier

Pay attention to the tension, beginning to be released in your body.

Look ahead of you and you will see a beautiful, brilliant, white glittering light coming towards you.

Breathe in deeply now and feel the energy coming towards you. Feel the softness and the peace coming closer to you. Feel this now become a part of you inside your body.

Breathe in deeply again. Become comfortable with this feeling of the divine light.

Breathe in and let the breath out slowly as you relax into the peace offered to you.

You will now begin to feel you are floating and moving off your chair.

As you begin to float, look up and see the sky opening and the rays of light coming to offer you the support you need to climb higher.

ANGEL TALK / CHATTING WITH THE ANGELS

As you go through the opening of the heavens you will notice the light shining before you.

Walk towards this wonderful light. Walk through the mist of the light and see the hand that presents itself to you.

As you reach out in faith to take this hand you suddenly become aware of the Angel's energy. When you have taken this hand you will be beckoned to come along and fly with your Angel.

You feel yourself being lifted into the air and holding on to the Angel.

You can see your Angel clearly now and know that you can now take this ride through the Universe.

Take your time now to enjoy your ride and notice all of the pictures and scenes around you. Take as much time as you need to listen to the sounds around you and record them into your memory. You will remember, all of the details of this journey when you arrive back.

(Take about 5-10 minutes for this part of the journey.)

Your Angels will now bring you back and set you down safely. They leave you with a feeling of safety and peace inside your mind and heart.

MEDITATION #2: MEETING YOUR PERSONAL ANGEL

Once you have arrived back to the opening in the sky and you begin to leave this area, the Angel takes your hand and places a beautiful gift in your hand.

Bring this gift back to your room, open it and see what your gift is.

Write about this in a journal. This gift is something you need at this time. It will help to heal from your past so that you have the ability to move forward, with a different outlook on life."

The Angels Speak Out

SECTION FOUR

SECTION FOUR: THE ANGELS SPEAK OUT

"ANGELS OF MINE"

"Angels divine Angels of mine

Where would you go, to bring in your glow?

Speak ever so clear, speak ever so clear,

To make the difference in a world

and bring in the good cheer!"

Madrina   February 23, 2009

SECTION FOUR: THE ANGELS SPEAK OUT

"Ride the waves of the light of God's love and we will carry you far."

From the Angel of Abundance

July 1, 2002

Dear Angels do you have a message tonight?

> "Christine dear sweet child of God, there is so much waiting out here for you! Come and get it! Open your mind, heart and soul it is here ready and waiting. Picture it all. Will it to you and pull it towards you. Surround yourself in this Light and bring it around all that is. We will bless you. Ask God to bless it and it will become a wonderful blessing for you. This is a very special gift from God!"

I have found that some of these messages took more than one evening to write out with all that they wanted to say to me about a topic.

ANGEL TALK / CHATTING WITH THE ANGELS

The next evening this Angel again gave me another message on this same topic.

*T*he Angel of Abundance

I heard these words and I began to wonder about what was being said. In the past I had worked with the light, that the angel were talking about. I just did not see the results as much as I felt I could have seen. It is hard to write about it from this perspective. I asked for clarification on this topic. This is the information that has followed since this message in the year 2002.

July 2, 2002

> "Oh Christine, so little time, time is so short! Short in the way of things are coming together quickly. The Light is bright. Brilliantly shining, such a Heavenly sight! Behold the Light! This shines for others to see. This shines to radiate to things for your highest good.
>
> This shines so brilliantly to knock down any obstacles or barriers! Allow the Light to grow even brighter.
>
> Play with this light and see it grow and watch it return to you. Watch and see what the light returns to you.
>
> Practice this and light the way for others to see this working. Shine the Light brighter than ever.

SECTION FOUR: THE ANGELS SPEAK OUT

Picture your hopes and desires and place this into the Light. Do this with something concrete for the first time to see what happens.

Once you see that this works, you will know it works. Start to place all of your cares, worries, needs, wants, desires, hopes and dreams into this Light. Send the Light out to retrieve this with the instructions to return this to you with a blessing from God.

These instructions are given with a small warning. DO NOT abuse this gift. This is to help you with your life and to be used to help others. You are trusted with the Light. We trust that you will instruct others to use this Light for the highest and the best for their lives.

These are the terms that are used with this work, Lightbearers, Lightkeepers, Lightweavers or Lightworkers. We hear these names often. We acknowledge these names are given to those who work with the Light of God. We send out our approval and ask that they continue to be used.

Record what you put into the light and keep a record of when and how it arrives back to you. Keep track of what your desires are and watch as these needs are all taken care of.

You can also find that you are washed from needing that desired thing any longer.

Some things will happen immediately and others will take more time to be accomplished. This is according to the balance and flow of this desire.

You must always keep a balance to keep the flow coming to you. Then you must give out in return. We will direct you with this and show you how this is to be.

Meditate with the Light of Abundance then watch and learn as time passes. You will learn what is needed here for our book of instructions on this topic.

This is the light of God's love and divine intervention of time and space. It is a God force to be used for the good of the Nation for Peace. You can put people into this light force and watch it change them and the situation for the better.

This is a Healing Light, Prosperity Light, and a Light for Peace. This Light shines all over the world. Tranquility! This is a Liquid Light for all to use, watch as it grows as you use it. It is never ending. It has an abundant supply that will continue to grow for eternity."

    Your Band of Angels, by the Angel of Abundance

SECTION FOUR: THE ANGELS SPEAK OUT

September 15, 2002

The Angel of Abundance says the following:

"How to Manifest a Miracle"

1. "Define your intention.

2. Be specific about what you want or desire.

3. Believe it is true.

4. Live it as if it has already happened.

5. Always find something to smile about it will radiate happiness inside. Remember that Happiness begins in the heart center and grows from there.

6. Always remember to be Grateful!

7. Give back to the Universe by helping others in some way.

8. Use positive thoughts and write affirmations.

Ex: I am healthy, happy and whole and so it is. I am full of life and have all in life that is needed at this time to fulfill my needs. I only need today that which I have today and all else is already in divine order.

Picture it all as energy of life. This energy is your divine source and is already a part of every cell in your being."

ANGEL TALK / CHATTING WITH THE ANGELS

October 15, 2003

Angel of Prosperity

Today is my mother's birthday so I send my love to you mom!

Once again I hear from the Angel of Prosperity. I have been hearing so much from this Angel. I guess there is so much to say about this topic. I figure that this Angel has so much to share, after all this is prosperity. The Universe has a never ending supply and so this Angel has an abundance of information to share with us.

So, sit back, relax, open your ears to listen and open your eyes to fill your mind with the words from this loving Angel. This Angel also gives us another wonderful meditation with the light.

Hello Dear Children of God,

"Today we ask that you go into the bible and look up the Beatitudes. Look and see that there are so many teachings. Listen and learn, because these Beatitudes will show the many blessings. The word Beatitudes is blessing or happy.

People tend to think that money is the only form of Prosperity. Prosperity is the gift from our God to you. The earth is filled with prosperity. There is so much more than people see. Look outside and see the richness of the world. Appreciate all of the beauty.

SECTION FOUR: THE ANGELS SPEAK OUT

Look around you and feel the Prosperity. Yes you can feel it! This feeling becomes a part of you. We ask that you never let go of it once you can find the wonderful experience of it.

When you fill your mind, heart, soul and body with it, you become alive. This feeling becomes satisfaction with life. You are whole and one with the spirit.

Meditate on filling your life with Prosperity and becoming one with the spirit of our God, with your God.

Practice the following Meditation. This will bring in the feeling of the colors of the light of prosperity. Take on this light and let it become a part of you. It will fill you with the energy of prosperity until you become the energy of a magnet, absorbing the light of prosperity. This is a never ending flooding of the light energy of prosperity."

*M*editation #3: *The Light and Feeling of Prosperity*

1. "Sit and relax take two deep breaths and release all the tension from your body and mind.

2. Imagine this wonderful color, the light of peacock green coming in and mixing with a light of a golden ray of light.

3. Feel this mixing and swirling, filling you from the top of your head down to your feet.

4. Once it reaches your feet, picture this light expanding out of your body, pulsating slowly and gradually expanding, then suddenly exploding filling you with Peace and contentment.

This peace is an eternal peace, filling your heart, mind, soul and body. It is the prosperity that will draw to you, all that you need in life.

5. Focus on this and allow it to bring to you what you need.

6. Believe this will happen, practice it, believe and be thankful.

7. Fill yourself with the Thankfulness.

8. Watch the happenings occur though out your life."

Meditation #3: The Light and Feeling of Prosperity

"The Colors of Life"

"As we walk this path, this lifetime,

we see much, hear much and live fully.

But do we absorb much?

Do we absorb all the beauty of Life?

All around experience the Colors of Life!

The passionate purples, intense blues,

vivacious yellows, crazy reds, precarious oranges!

Smell the colors of life!

What are the colors and how do they smell

after a wonderfully refreshing spring rain?

Does a rainbow of colors appear only in a rainbow?

SECTION FOUR: THE ANGELS SPEAK OUT

How do the colors feel after a freshly fallen crispy snowstorm?

Have you lived until you have plunged into

the rippling cool waters on a hot summer's day?

Can you experience the colors of life?

Think about the days and nights.

Watch as your day turns into night.

Experience the stillness of the night

and the colors of the evening

with the glistening stars in the sky.

As you lay your head down to say goodnight,

Breathe deeply and take in the colors of your life."

Madrina

Write about your experiences with Meditation #3:

SECTION FOUR: THE ANGELS SPEAK OUT

July 8, 2008   1:22 AM

Angels of Knowledge

Hello Angels,

I hear your conversations tonight. I hear you talking about attracting things to you. So I ask you to show me more clearly how to work with this energy in a more productive way.

> Dear Christine,
>
> "We will tell you in a very plain and simple way, what happens with the Law of Attraction. People say they are trying to attract things to them such as money, cars, love, etc. One of the main things that people must remember is, all of these things are energy.
>
> We ask you to realize that all of the energy in the world is already present right where you are. When you have recognized this fact, then you have made the first step in accomplishing attraction.
>
> First ask for what you want. Make it very specific. Then you can focus on that object and have a heart of gratitude for what is already there. Put a time on what you want. Say I would like to see something manifest within one week, wait and see what happens.

Start with something small, work your way up to bigger things and see what happens.

One of the things that can get in the way of something coming along is someone's belief system. Do you believe deep down inside that this works? Do you believe that you are worthy of receiving it?

It then comes from, how bad do you want this item and can you let go of the wanting of this? Once you have asked for it do not keep going back to ask again and again. That tells God that you really do not believe you can have it.

Start to believe that this is something that you can have! There is no reason that you can not have things in this world. God made things for your enjoyment.

If you keep asking and asking for something it starts the whole process over again. You only have to ask once and then let it go.

Do not believe that because someone else does not have things or there is so much poverty out there, that you can not possibly have these things. Please feel good about receiving it. Always feel good about receiving.

That is a very important key to all of this. To feel good about what you do receive. Feel good about what you have asked for and you will receive.

SECTION FOUR: THE ANGELS SPEAK OUT

If you do not receive exactly the way you asked for it, investigate how you asked for it. Ask yourself what you perceived you would get. If everything seems to fit together, then realize that God knew better than you about what you really needed at that time in your life.

Sometimes God will look and see that you could use a new car versus a trip. So sometimes your prayers get answered for your highest and best even though it just does not seem so at the time.

Most importantly remember to believe that you deserve it and that you can have it. There are so many who do not believe that they will receive things. God's precious gifts are many in this world. It is all in God's energy that these things do exist.

Hopefully we have told you this in a simpler manner and you can utilize this information better.

Believe and be open to receive and it will come to you. It is already present, just stay open and allow it to flow to you. Be open to receive whatever it is that you want in your life. Do not want it more than you can handle, just ask and believe that is the most important thing. Feel grateful and stay in that gratitude energy."

Your Angels of Knowledge

My husband and I have been shown this new energy from the Angels. We have really been playing with this new energy over the past few weeks and have had some very interesting reactions with it. It is hard sometimes to put this all into action but I know something worked for the last few weeks for us because of these things.

I had heard from the Angels to ask for what I needed. My husband and I needed a new mattress really bad. Ours was so bad that it was hurting my husband's back and we wanted a certain mattress. We had been looking for about three weeks. We decided to pay only cash for what we wanted and so we saved our money. When we went shopping at the stores for the mattress nothing was within our price range of the cash we had on hand. I knew this would be a great thing to work on using the Law of Attraction.

I told the Angels that we had to have a high quality King Size Memory Foam mattress before the week was out. I also told them that the price needed to be within the amount of money I had in cash.

The very next day I heard to go look at a certain site on the Internet and there would be what we needed there. Sure enough I went to this site and there were two mattresses at this site for sale.

We called on them both. One was only one month old and only had been slept on for about a week. We were told they were only replacing it because the woman was used to a different brand of mattress than this one.

SECTION FOUR: THE ANGELS SPEAK OUT

We went right over that evening to look at it. When we saw it we were so excited! It really was brand new! We laid on it and it was perfect. Not only was it in excellent condition, the price they were asking was exactly what I had saved! We did purchase it that day. It was considerably less than the mattresses we had been looking at in the stores. We saved money in the long run purchasing this one. It is so nice to have the mattress and my husband's back no longer hurts him.

I decided to begin practicing with this concept of the time limit and being more specific on what we needed in our life. I then just let go and began working at listening very closely.

Angel of Abundance with the Energy Ball of Light

Angel Message for September 2008

Dear Children of the Light,

"We come to you today to ask that each of you start your September in a new energy. Claim this new energy as your way and light. This will bring in the energy needed for the completion of a cycle for each person, who calls in the **Energy Ball of the Light** to work with in your personal lives.

This **Energy Ball of the Light** is to be used for the highest and the best.

For those who feel trapped in life it will bring to you a new release of trapped energy. It will clear out the debris that is left over in your system and allow your energy to flow.

This will bring in higher positive charges of electrical pulses that will jump-start any projects you have been contemplating. It will bring about a pulse of energy that will bring with it a high vibration of energy. You will feel the surge coming to you very quickly.

Balance this new energy with positive thought patterns. Put them together with determination. Watch as this brings to you the necessary tools needed, to bring about the completions of projects in your life.

SECTION FOUR: THE ANGELS SPEAK OUT

If you need to bring about a new job opportunity, put that thought to the light, bring in the **Energy Ball of the Light**. Focus on it. Claim it with determination. Then release the outcome with belief that it is already here. See it grow! Watch in your mind as it comes to you. See yourself working in the environment you want to be in.

Build the picture and feel the happiness you have created and what the energy has brought to you.

Be grateful for the surges of energy and watch it work in your life. Do not give up, keep moving forward and believe it will happen. Do not change your thought on it or the idea will take longer to come about. Keep things focused, the details crisp, the energy on a high vibration and you will notice it moves much more steadily.

Do not quit now, keep moving forward and smile brightly. Know that we have this covered and are grateful to be working with the Universe on this project for all of you. It is our privilege to be called in to do the Universal Light work.

We leave you now with a project of hope. Light the world each day by sending out a huge ball of light into the world. See this light surround all the beings in this world. Send this out with the deep seeded Love of God. Know that it will bring about a great healing to your Nations."

Your Band of Angels joined together to bring forth the **Energy Ball of Light** to all in need!

*A*ngel of Poverty

Angels are all around traveling to our plain to help us achieve peace in our lives. They are here to teach us higher learning and life lessons.

June 21, 2008

The lesson tonight is about poverty.

"Poverty is not something that people of this world should tolerate. There is abundance everywhere. Poverty is a state of being. It is a state of being amongst those who need to be lifted. People need to learn this lesson of abundance they need to want better than what they have.

Take time to help those in need as much as you can. There is hope for those without in this world. The hope is, God's Love and Light. The hope is that the love will lift them higher and higher. It will bring them the peace they so deserve. The feeling of being worthy of deserving is one of the obstacles that we will work on from this side.

SECTION FOUR: THE ANGELS SPEAK OUT

This will help those in need to overcome this feeling of being unworthy. The feeling of self worth is another obstacle that others can help the ones in need overcome.

We ask for others to help us in the battle of poverty and we dream of overcoming these situations in the world.

We ask for people to talk about this poverty. Talk about the need to conquer it. Make it a strong display of knowledge to other countries and the people of this world.

Education is one of the keys to the conquering of Poverty. Educate the People on how to grow abundant in what is needed in their world. Teach them also how to find the peace and happiness they so deserve.

Not all values of life are the same everywhere. Some need much less to be happy. Some think they need so much more than really is needed to be happy.

Find your balance and then teach others to find theirs. Poverty is a state of being we say again. Find your state of being. Bring it balance and harmony so you can live in the abundance of life.

Law of Attraction with the Angel of Abundance

Putting it all together

There is a lot of information in the Angel messages over the years about the Law of Attraction. I really did argue with the Angels on writing more about the Law of Attraction because there is so much out there on this topic.

Well, you see who won! I should have known better by now! Whenever I am asked to do something, I should just do it. It usually comes out much better with much less effort if I just do as I am asked. I just believe I need to question things sometimes. This helps me to make sure I am hearing them right and with the appropriate guidance on the different topics.

I will give this information the way I am directed. It is my wish that it can help as many people out there that need this type of help. This time with our world situation as it is, I believe we are all in need of this information.

Sometimes I think we work way too hard on this Law of Nature. The Law of Attraction works whether you use it or not. It works to the fullest potential. It works in a way that either you enjoy what is going on or you are frustrated trying to figure out what you are doing wrong.

SECTION FOUR: THE ANGELS SPEAK OUT

What I would like to do, with the guidance of the Angels, is break this down. I will tell you what I have been hearing and working with over this last year especially with this Law of Nature.

I have asked for help with this particular Law in my life. Over the last few years, it has been tough for my husband and me financially. I wanted to see how I could work with Natural Law and see what I could change over time in our lives.

It seems to be an awaking time for us. Stan and I are learning so much we want to share our experiences with you.

The Angels now tell us to,

> "First and foremost find out what you want in life and be prepared to let go of all that is not working. Make sure you understand what working means to you. This definition is different in each eye! What may be working for you may not appear that way to someone else."

Stan and I realized that we needed to make some major changes We had to begin this process with letting go of our farm. That meant letting go of our horses and a lot of other possesions. That was the hardest struggle for almost a full year. Through out this time we chose to turn things over to God. We made room in our life for more prayer and meditation. We were trying to find answers to the dilemma we found ourselves in. While it was difficult to go through, it proved to be a time of amazement also. We found various answers to things happening in our lives and grew so much spiritually

Several years ago we asked God to allow us to be debt free and living independent lives. That was answered with this move. Letting go of so many of our things, made it difficult to make decisions on what had to go and what we needed to keep. With letting go so much, we no longer had the responsibility of a whole lot.

With our children moving on with their lives, we are no longer as responsible for them. Our grandchildren have now moved to different states and we do not have them living as close. We did not quite mean that we did not want the responsibility of our children and grandchildren. I guess it is all a package deal.

We do get time to travel to see the families and love our time together. We miss them all when we are not with them. I realized though, that our children had their own agenda and is different from what we had asked for. The outcome of what you ask for can be changed, when it does involve someone else's life. There are many more free wills that can be affected by what you asked for. So the first one to be answered will be the one that most concerns you and your situation.

We have seen through the answers to the prayers and messages from the Angels, that for us, this is a healing time. It is also a time to recover from the struggles of trying to maintain our life the way it was. It is a time to re-evaluate what is important to us in our lives.

SECTION FOUR: THE ANGELS SPEAK OUT

Our family is the most important to us. Next is our independence with our businesses which is important so we can continue to do what God has asked of me to accomplish. These are our gifts and we felt we needed to accomplish them.

We continue to grow our businesses; my husband Stan's stained glass studio **"Norwood Custom Glass"** in Cincinnati, Ohio is growing.

I am working on some new programs to bring to the public as well as doing the Spiritual Counseling and Grief Counseling. With the help of the Angels guiding us in God's way, we are experiencing so much growth and learning along the way.

We had asked for a business to be brought to us that would grow and bring us an income that would help us have more freedom and be able to travel. I had one that was not moving forward as I had hoped it would.

I had decided to put this energy to it and use what I had been taught. I put together a list of things I wanted to have happen with a time frame. Within just a few months I had put together a wonderful presentation on this product and had things printed up thinking this was the business that was going to take off.

I will tell you within just a few months, another business presented itself in such a way that I could not just walk away. It is Healthy Chocolate!

Everything, and I mean everything that I had put on my list happened within the first few weeks of being introduced to this new business. I had shown this to Stan, some of my family and friends. They agreed with me that we needed to take a chance and do this business. Our Healthy Chocolate business began with my brother Mike and sister-in-law Andie. It has been a great adventure for the four of us! It is allowing us to have fun meeting new people.

I still today feel this is a blessing from God and the opportunity presents itself when it is most needed.

So much is happening in my life since I found this meditation and the method of the Ball of Light. Every time something else happens I just stand there and I smile. I then think Wow it has happened again! It just warms my heart.

When things slow down a bit, I am much calmer when I do not see something I think I am supposed to do or know. It is as the Angels said; you will either receive it or the need of whatever it was will be taken away. Sometimes I have found that the need comes back again and then whatever it was shows up.

SECTION FOUR: THE ANGELS SPEAK OUT

February. 20, 2009

Here is what the Angels have to say about this in life.

> "Life can be very interesting once you stop and pay attention to it. Watch as things begin to unfold. Begin to pay attention so you learn to become aware of what is happening. Do not try to dissect it at every turn, you will drive yourself crazy! Just allow it.
>
> You can work on trying to understand, it is good to learn. If it does not make sense let it go, release the outcome, allow the process to unfold. Enjoy the ride of life, you will experience many more smiles.
>
> Life is an experience of all sorts of emotions, such as: laughter, joy, fear, sadness and there are many other emotions. Just know that you can experience them all. There is another side to each one and you will reach the other side of the worst and the best.
>
> Walk through this time and watch as we teach you along the way Do not always think you are being tested. Think instead that you are learning as you go. Some lessons are harder if you have more to learn and will be used to help others one day. Other lessons seem to carry you along the way. Just realse and allow!
>
> Ride the waves of the light of God's love and we will carry you far.

Take just a few minutes, to jot down ideas and thoughts about what you are experiencing now in your life. Write down the emotion that goes hand in hand with it. Write down the opposite opposite of this and see where you are in this time of your life.

Appreciate right where you are. If you are not happy with what is happening right now in your life, picture the opposite and claim it. Once you have done this, add it to God's light of love and allow the changes to flow to you.

Wait for your experiences in life and appreciate the journey along the way. God is preparing you for what is the highest and the best in your lifetime. Prepare yourself to receive this delightful experience.

With Honor and Respect,"

    Your Angel of Abundance with Abundant life!

SECTION FOUR: THE ANGELS SPEAK OUT

*A*ngel of Humor

Angels remind us to keep things simple in life because it is the simple things that are the important things. It is in the simple things of our everyday life that we can find humor.

It is like watching the sea gulls at the beach. They bother a lot of people most of the time. So many people may not find the humor in them. I watched people throwing sticks at them to make them go away. It was funny to watch the gulls and their reaction. They would dive at the sticks and play in the air with these sticks. They would then drop them back down at the people. These gulls were not threatened in the least bit. It almost seemed like they just wanted to play and have fun with the people. Unfortunately, people missed the adventure of the playfulness of the Sea Gull!

I watched them with a humorous attitude while on vacation. They just made me laugh with their playful attitudes. If you would toss just one little piece of food in the air, not just one would fly over, but all of the gulls in the area would come flying in for a landing. They flew in just to see which one could get that one little piece of food. The one that got the food seemed to prance around showing off, while the others would start to squawk at it in protest.

This is just one way to find your Angels of Humor. Begin to look through different eyes, at situations that might just normally bother you, to the point of frustration and even anger. You can look at the situation and find some humor in it or something humorous around it. The gulls were having fun, some people were not, but I just started to watch them play. I began to watch them closer and see that they had no cares they were free to play. It is up to us to decide that is what we want to do.

I will say, I know you cannot find humor in everything or every situation in life. I know that myself through some of our tough times. No ones life is peaches and cream all of the time. It is through these times when you try to walk with the Holy Spirit and the Angels, they will help you get through to the other side of that situation.

Nothing is hopeless when you have the amount of help we receive from God. When you go through your dark times, always remember there is help from the other side. There is a light at the end of that tunnel, just waiting for you to see it and let it guide you along the way.

The Angels of Humor tells me,

"The dark times represent a death to a certain time or things in your life and you will be reborn a new person having gone through it.

SECTION FOUR: THE ANGELS SPEAK OUT

Sometimes the dark times are learning times. These times are when you need a change or something different in your life needs to change.

There are times you have had lots of warnings but ignore them, other times you are oblivious to them. The situations are allowed to occur to move us forward in life. You can decide to try to listen, grow and move on without a lot of turmoil. It is easier and definitely a lot more fun!

We are aware, there are some sad things that occur for what seems there are no apparent reasons.

We are here to tell you that in almost every circumstance, there will be some sort of humor put into your life. This will help to get you through anything you are going through.

Just open your eyes so you can see it. Keep your mind clear so you can focus on it when it is presented to you, as the precious gift it is meant to be.

Laughter is the best medicine for most anything. We are telling you and ask you to believe it. It is amazing how much just a simple smile will help people who see it. Take the time to give a smile along the way. You might just find that you will receive one back at just the perfect time when you need it the most."

This is the ending comment for the Angel of Humor.

"Humor is the cure for so many things. Find your Humor and you just might find the cure for what is bothering you most today. You might just find that hidden smile!"

*A*ngel of Compassion

September 11, 2003

This was the second Anniversary of the 911 attacks on the United States. I said a prayer for all of the family members and friends of those killed in the 911 attacks. I was not sleeping very well at all. I was tossing and turning most of the night and kept hearing different voices crying out. There were a lot of loud noises in the night. I decided to get up and write to the Angels to find out what was happening. I asked the Angels tonight what they wanted to teach me. I was told the following:

> Our dearest children of God,
>
> "We come tonight to talk about Compassion. Having compassion is easy; you should not have to work at it. Most humans have this naturally, most of the time, but sometimes you do forget about it.

SECTION FOUR: THE ANGELS SPEAK OUT

Compassion for your fellow person is something you will need to help others do, by having it yourself. Smile at people. Do not be afraid to help. If you see someone who needs help, *Please* help him or her! Open the door, say God Bless you, Excuse Me, Sorry, etc.

Begin first with going into your own heart center and allowing this center to open to Love. Once it is open to love, compassion will follow. Focus on all mankind. Send Love and Compassion out to them. Ask God to bless each and every person on the earth good, bad or indifferent! Thank God for these blessings.

Now go out each day and be aware of those you can practice compassion on. The woman struggling with a child and bags, offer to help open a door or anything you see you can do. If you see someone trying to find something they lost ask if they need help.

Have a listening ear and a closed mouth to others.

Take compassion one-step closer. Actually feel the compassion in your heart for others. Now describe what you feel, understand and except these feelings and use them every day.

Compassion is an action that each person should try to put into practice on a daily basis. It will begin to lead to peace within families, then reach out across the oceans and touch the world."

Love and Light

Your Angel of Compassion

*A*ngel of Peace

September 16, 2003 Tuesday

"Angels, Angels, Angels fly free be ready always, Christine fly free. Let go of the life you think you have to live, in the manner you think is important. Ask us for direction, then listen and watch as things begin to unfold.

This course has already begun, since you committed to working for us. Remember to trust what is told to you. This is important to trust us.

We know that we work for our God for the good of mankind. The world and all of the people there are important to us. We are assigned to help the people begin to open their hearts and their eyes. Through our teachings, we will help to Create World Peace.

> Honesty is Key to Peace. Being honest with you first, is a key element to beginning the process of opening the heart to God.
>
> Feel all of your feelings and work on each emotion coming from within. Open your mind to accept whatever you feel there. Once you are true to yourself and love yourself then honesty will come along much easier."
>
> The Angel of Peace

Angels of Peace and Joy

October 17, 2003 Friday

It is 12:35 A.M. and tonight the Angels of Peace and Joy want to talk to the world.

> "It is when you find true Peace in your heart, that you will experience true Inner Joy throughout your entire body. It then radiates out into the world and spreads Joy all over the world.
>
> How do you find that inner peace you may ask? The simplest or easiest way is, to ask us to help you find it. Then you will understand that it is so.
>
> Be grateful that we have heard your plea. Know we have brought it before our God and presented it to this most wonderful energy.

Except that everything and everybody is exactly where it should be in life.

Believe this to be true. Remember all of you have a free will. Be free to experience true Peace and Joy.

Now comes the part that is the hardest thing. That is being human, having emotions or conflicting thoughts about this whole topic and not understanding.

Let us explain that this is a daily thing. It is something to do every day. Remember to be grateful for the experiences you have had, the people who have come in and out of your life, and for all of the things you have.

The more Thankful you can be for all of these things the more Peace you will experience.

Count your blessings and do not add up the misfortunate experiences of the things you lack. Some days they may out weigh the things to be grateful for.

When you feel you have nothing else to be grateful for, try practicing being grateful for the new day when you wake up. Then upon retiring at night be grateful for the day you had the privilege to experience.

This way you will begin and end each new day with a grateful heart.

SECTION FOUR: THE ANGELS SPEAK OUT

Practice this lesson, keep it foremost in your mind and use it when times get tough. When it is too tough to handle you can be grateful for the smallest of smallest things. The touch of a little tiny baby's hand, the smile from some little child's face, a little puppy dogs funny waddle, the nod of a head, the song of a bird, the sunshine or the fresh smell of rain.

Go through your day looking for things to be grateful for by doing this daily.

One day you will find that true Inner Peace, which in turn leads to that true Joy.

It all sounds so easy but it is through practice that you succeed at this.

So practice Peace and Joy, you will enjoy it once you find it. Guaranteed!!!

Go now in Peace and joy!"

Your Band of Angels of Peace and Joy

October 19, 2003 Saturday

*A*ngel of Transformation

Tonight the Angel of Transformation will speak. Some call this Angel the Angel of Death. This Angel says,"

> "I am called the Angel of Transformation because death is not death to anything, but a new beginning to life. It is another opportunity to grow and learn as well as to help others grow and learn. The struggles are here but lessened and are different"

This overwhelming feeling of awe comes over me as this Angel steps in closer and tells me to listen closely.

> "I am NOT an Angel of Darkness but of great light. If you do not actually see me it is good, because it is not your time to leave your realm. This is why so many see me in darkness. If I am here you may not look upon me or you will be leaving with me.
>
> There is much I would like to teach on this topic so we will need much uninterrupted time to teach this. Understand you will have a better understanding about what death is to your world.

SECTION FOUR: THE ANGELS SPEAK OUT

It takes time for your body to prepare for this transformation. Even when it seems like your life ended here suddenly, your body, mind and spirit have been preparing for this time.

There is no such thing as sudden death to you from this side of things.

There are so many issues with this topic and so much to say in order for the people not to have fear when this time comes.

You continually transform through life. Death is only the final transformation of your human body in this lifetime.

First thing we wish to teach is, God has sent so much help to you, to live your life to the fullest. We ask you to remember that you have the Angels, Guides, Loved Ones from here, and people around you as you live on earth. There is so much guidance given to you. Why would you be left alone when your transformation occurs?

There are many here, preparing the way for you. Many Angels light the way. Your family and friends on this side, come to welcome you. Your guides are here to help prepare for your transition. Then we have many who work from the earth planes that we have trained to help you from your end, if you get caught up in old beliefs to be stranded in your world.

> We have more and more help out there for you. We pick the assistants who will be assigned to help you come to our side of life. We know they are dedicated to helping. Once over on this side you can return to do more light work of the world.
>
> People get so stuck in their beliefs when in the living. It gets very difficult to let go of their bodies once they leave them.
>
> They can not accept that things will be just fine. They stay where they either feel safe or have familiar feelings. They can also get caught up in how they transformed from this earth plane. They will then reenact it over and over again, until the pattern can be broken. They can then be lead over to our side of life."

Monday Oct. 20, 2003

Tonight this energy is very hard for me to hear. This energy is on a much higher vibration. It is so high that it creates such an inner peace. I almost do not hear anything, I can just feel it. I then hear the following:

> "Ahhhh, and now Christine you understand the message tonight. We fight our body's death so much we stay tense about it and we fight it so much we forget to be at Peace.
>
> This is what this transformation is about, finding a true inner peace about us.

SECTION FOUR: THE ANGELS SPEAK OUT

> We would like people to understand and feel this true peace for the person getting ready for or preparing for their transformation from this plane, to the next dimension of life.
>
> We need people who are around these souls that are getting ready to make this transition, to help them prepare for this great peace, by allowing them the freedom to leave. Everyone around at this time will then benefit from this same feeling of peacefulness."

The Angel of God' Blessings and Transformation

This is the information the Angel of Transformation asked me to include in this book about the dying process.

Angel of Happiness

September 18, 2003

> Angels I keep hearing you say, "Happiness, Happiness, True Happiness is only found deep inside your own self. It comes from your heart center. It is not always easy to see or feel. It is not always easy to obtain true heartfelt happiness throughout life.
>
> Our best advice about this is to not let all of the little things bog you down. Handle the big situations in life as they come along.

Learn from them and move on. Do not take all of the negative energy from any situation and keep it or hang on to it forever. Let it Go!

Allow yourself to learn from every experience in life. Always remember God has not left you here to walk the path of life alone. He has sent many helpers into your life.

Now it is up to you to bring that Inner Peace and Joy of Happiness into your heart."

MEDITATION #4: WARMING OF A HAPPY HEART

Meditation #4: Warming of a Happy Heart:

"1. Allow God's love for you to enter and warm your whole being. Send this warmth to your Heart Center and allow it to work its way out into the rest of your body.

2. Focusing inside, write down the things that make you unhappy, then meditate on these items and release them, releasing all of the emotions that go with them.

3. Now write about all of the things that make you happy or have given you Peace and Joy inside. It can be your children, any family or an event. You can experience the joy of watching the wonders of the world, such as a spider spinning it's web. You can do this by sitting by the water or laying on the ground, enjoying the blue sky on a quiet cool day. These are just a few ideas.

4. Now it is your turn to take this time to list some of the things that do not make you smile, but will bring that joy clear down deep inside your whole being.

5. Capture that emotion and feeling you now feel. Hold it near and dear.

Remember it is always there for you, whenever you need a pick me up or a bit of a refresher course in happiness. You can always grab it back again, whenever you need it, if you can hold onto that feeling.

Once you can teach yourself to carry this inner glow, be ready because it will then start to flow out of you and touch others deep inside them also!

Work with this process and do not give up! Sometimes we get so caught up in our life we forget to feel that Happiness and it gets lost. So cherish this Happiness like a Treasure, because it is a wonderful gift from God."

SECTION FOUR: THE ANGELS SPEAK OUT

Write about your experience with Meditation #4:

Angel of Fear

September 19, 2003 Friday

"Fear, what about fear you might ask. Some people say to fear God. We ask you, what should be feared about God. We know our God well and we are the Army for God! We do not fear this energy!

We only fear that people will not listen and will not start the changes within themselves that will then lead to lighting the torch for God's light to live brightly amongst all human beings.

Love God with all of your hearts and do good for others, then you will not need to fear our God.

Fear in another way is something people feel, when changes in their life comes. Once again when you ask for God's help you need not fear your path. Know and believe your prayers have been heard.

God sends so much help. We Angels are here for the purpose of helping humans. Your Spirit Guides also are here to help. You only need to ask us for help! We are so glad to come and assist you.

SECTION FOUR: THE ANGELS SPEAK OUT

Everyone has a free will. We cannot intervene in your free will. This is why you need to ask us. This then gives us your permission to intervene and help you on your life's journey. We get so excited when we get to work with those on the Earth Plain. It is our honor to do this work for our God.

We also can pray for each of you as well as intervene with God for you.

We believe that each one of you can make the changes necessary to save your world from the destruction going on right now

It only takes a few to light the torch of God's light and let it burn bright from you, to lead others into God's Light.

We call out now to challenge each one that reads this, to answer the call and help us fight this battle for our God!

We thank you for your help and send many blessings in return. We can get rid of the fear so many face in their lives, once we change the hearts of people. When that happens, then people will start to answer this call and fear can be replaced by Love!

Fear comes from the unknown but sometimes from knowing. Knowing what to do but not how to do it or make it happen.

Fear of the unknown is the anticipation of what is to come.

Turn it all over and allow us to work on your behalf. We only have your best interest in our hearts. We will take your fears to our God. The God energy wants to bless each of you with the Love from our Mother / Father God. This energy will bless you to the depths of your soul."

SECTION FOUR: THE ANGELS SPEAK OUT

An Angel Blessing:

"Close your eyes and picture whatever is troubling you. Put it all out into the open. Hand it over into our hands. Watch these things pass from your mind, heart, soul and body. Watch and feel us take these things from you and take them to God.

Feel the presence of our Lord. This warm highly powered energy is so refreshing, powerful and loving you can not stay with it very long and yet you can not stay away from it very long either. You will crave more of it.

We allow you to experience it briefly to feel the overwhelming cleansing from the situation, problems or any concerns you just released. We ask you now to allow us to take it to our God on your behalf.

Now feel the peace, joy and contentment from having released this burden. Remember to release other things to us as they occur, then it relieves you from the burden of carrying all of this with you for so long.

Then you can release the fear that builds up inside.

Go now in Peace and Joy with God's Blessings bestowed upon you and the world."

> The Angels of God's light and love in charge of Fear

Angel of Patience

September 21, 2003 Sunday

"Patience, patience is something people always say, do not ask for that!

Well this is true and the main thing to remember is that this is something that all people already have. It is not something you have to practice. Patience is something you have inside yourself. You were born with it. So many gifts that each one is blessed with! This is one of many!

It is hard sometimes to remember that you have this gift when things are not going in the direction you feel they should or you need to wait for something or someone. This happens especially when someone is doing something that frustrates you.

The mere practice of remembering that Patience is a gift and the fact that you possess this gift, will help you use it, over and over again without even realizing you are using it.

Be ever so thankful for Patience, this is one of the strongest and most used gifts God has given each of you.

SECTION FOUR: THE ANGELS SPEAK OUT

It is just in the simple act of sending someone a blessing when they do something to test your patience, which will result in it coming back to you many times in rewards. It may happen in ways you may never realize is a reward! So many blessings are sent so do not take God's gifts for granted, ever.

Anger can stimulate and disrupt the patience in anyone. So learn to not allow anger to control you or take over things in your life. You can feel the anger coming into your being but do not let it stay with you. Let it go as soon as you realize it is there. Just do a release technique and let it go. Never hold on to it very long. When you learn to let it go, then a healing occurs and your patience is something you are aware of again."

Angel of Trust

September 23, 2003 Tuesday

"Trust is the issue Christine. Trust in what you learn from us. Trust to the core of your being from your heart to God's heart. All truth lies there.

Follow your dream is the best advice. Go for what you believe to be true. When you feel happiness and joy in your heart, trust that you are being guided in the best direction. This is especially true if this joy and peace in your heart brings peace, joy and happiness to others in the long run.

We need strong warriors to be in this battle with us. Grow stronger everyday; keep the light burning by being at peace with joy and love in your heart. Feel us carrying you along the way. We are working with you daily and at night, to teach you how to let us work through you. This will help you feel more comfortable when this happens again.

Trust us to only bring good into your life and know we will never; never harm you in any manner. Believe we hear you and are guiding you along the way.

We have given you the keys to wisdom before as one of your gifts. What we teach in these chapters are the keys to understanding such wisdom.

SECTION FOUR: THE ANGELS SPEAK OUT

These are the keys to unlock the mysteries of living this lifetime. All that we are teaching now needs to be unlocked and exposed to others so the people will know and understand the truths of this way of living.

This is so important especially this time in the world with so much division and so much hatred of the humans of each other. God only sees love and goodness in the children that roam the earth.

All people are God's children and the God life sparks the Christ light. It is alive in each human and continues to live within. You are told that each person is made in the image and likeness of God.

Trust that this is the time to show others. Our hands are upon your head with blessings to clear out the confusion, frustration and impatience, hatred and anger. Our love for you will calm your fears and uncertainties."

Your Angels of God's Light of Trust.

The Angels wanted me to include the message about Trust in the book to let others know that God has sent the Angels to bring about a peace to the world. They will stand beside all those who answer the call to help by trusting these words to be true. The Angels send blessings to each of us and send the knowledge to understand these words and know they are true.

Angel of Faith

October 7, 2003 Tuesday

The next lesson from the Angels is on Faith.

"What do you have faith in and what is faith anyway? Well dear children faith is something you believe with all of your heart.

It is also something that you can transform from your heart into your mind to understand and except. So now we ask for you to have faith and believe that once asked, we will begin to work for your highest good.

Take your questions and request to bring them out. Put them into your heart and mind. Then understand that we have heard you and believe that we have immediately begun to work on them for you.

Do not take them back into your own heart and mind; again. This will bring them back to the earthly realm. We ask for you to leave these questions or requests in our hands and heart. Then transfer them to the Spiritual realm. This is where we can solve them with God's help. They will then be sent back with the answer or solutions."

Thank you for listening and allowing us to serve.

SECTION FOUR: THE ANGELS SPEAK OUT

February 10, 2009   Tuesday

As I am typing these words from the Angels from my notebook I am beginning to hear more on this lesson of Faith so I will include it now.

"Working on Faith is an issue many seem to have a problem with. From what we can tell from our perspective is that most people lack the faith in themselves, to be able to turn things over to God.

They believe that they have to do everything themselves. If you would just let things be, once you have put them in God's hands, we could work so much more efficiently on each issue. It is when you begin to doubt and wonder if anything is being heard or if there is an answer, the process from our end has to begin again.

So just let things go once you have released them to the power of God. Do not ask again. Let it rest in the knowledge that God is the best judge of things.

Have the faith that God will guide you along the way. The things you are to do will be shown clearly. Ask for clear vision and clear hearing. It will be there once you build your faith and believe it is there.

We know that people try their best and sometimes slip backwards.

That is okay, because we are there to catch you. We will put you back up on your feet to help you walk forward. We will carry you along the way.

We thank you for your trust in us and the faith that you have shown, to allow us to help you move forward with this work. We are guiding you with all of the work that you are doing in the world.

We thank each of you for doing God's work and for all that you are bringing to the world with your light shining bright.

God thanks you for shining your lights so brightly. We see sunny days ahead, and lots of hearts glowing bright in the light.

Great healings are taking place throughout the world as we speak here tonight.

We are grateful for those who will listen to these words and taking the time to apply them to their lives."

The Angels of God's Army

SECTION FOUR: THE ANGELS SPEAK OUT

Meditation #5:

Receiving messages from specific Angels

Sit in a comfortable place with a pad of paper and a pen or pencil.

Call on your Angel to bring in the Angel you wish to receive a message from.

Begin to write out the first words that come to your mind.

You can continue this as you call on different Angels to bring in messages for your personal, spiritual growth or the Universal growth for the world issues.

MEDITATION #5: MESSAGES FROM SPECIFIC ANGELS

Write about your experience with Meditation #5:

Universal Angel Messages

SECTION FIVE

SECTION FIVE: UNIVERSAL ANGEL MESSAGES

The World"

"The World needs change.

Change the world with Love

Love all beings and all creatures.

The Earth will brighten as love spreads.

Look through the eyes of Love.

See the bright light grow even brighter.

This all comes from shining the light of Love."

Madrina in 2003

"Life's a Ball, You Just Forgot How To Dribble It!"

Ariella 2008

Changing the way the Universal Energy Flows

The Angels have asked me to put some of these messages in a different category. They have asked me to list them as Universal Messages. They are for changing the way the Universal energy flows. We can change the universe, if everyone begins to listen. We need to utilize this new way of thinking and treating others, to become a more light-based world to live in.

It seems that ever since I started to hear these messages from the Angels, they have been asking us, to pray for the world.

SECTION FIVE: UNIVERSAL ANGEL MESSAGES

They want these prayers to go out to all of the people that are living in this world. The Angels are at battle trying to save all of the people and the world that God created for us to live in.

July 2, 2002

Earlier I wrote about the Angel of Abundance for the Ball of Liquid Light. I am now adding this in the Universal messages to finish the message given to me for the world that night.

> "Changes are coming nearer for the world. Wrap the Universe in this blanket of Light for protection. Send protection to the people.
>
> God is near. Do not let others frustrate you or discourage any of you from doing God's work. Follow your heart. We are there always to help you and support you. We are there even if you cannot see us, hear us or are not aware of us. Trust that we are not far away because we are holding you up. We are your support, always.
>
> Meditate, send out the Light and watch it return to you in Peace. Drape the Light around the people of the world and watch the heart center change. Only send out positive thoughts and actions. This will promote and encourage this action and bring it into the Universe stronger and stronger.
>
> Your Band of Angels

United together as your Shield of Armor!

Love to You and the World!

God speed!

Angel Message: August 1, 2002

I hear a song start and then, I hear the singing with the music. *"Angels, Angels, Angels, Angels."* I hear them continue to sing this over and over again. It brings such peace inside me to hear the choir of Angels sing. I hear this more and more as I begin to hear the Power of the Band of Angels come into our realm.

They begin by saying,

"Many need to hear this and hear our words. So many are hungry. They hunger for God's knowledge. They are so thirsty. We will quench their thirst and hunger! We will fill the void! Allow this to flow and Let the Light Shine! This brings about Peace and Harmony! The people will once again be filled with the Joy of Life!

We want others to feel us beside them. We ask for others to be aware, be aware of the changes within. Take time to stand with us.

Hang around with us and we will float you on the way! Walk beside us and let us carry you on this ride. Time is at hand to shine. The world needs the leaders.

SECTION FIVE: UNIVERSAL ANGEL MESSAGES

We are calling to all of the World Angels to unite. Unite now and stand strong together.

We call out louder! Louder! Louder! We call out to each of you to join together to create this band of earth World Angels. You are all hearing us, you are all calling out to us. Unite together now to go out through the entire world, collect each other and join together. The world of all nations, come together now and hear the calling of your names! Allow the followers to join up and stand tall.

Connect with each other and learn all that you can. Put together the puzzle pieces each of you have collected over time. You will then see the whole picture. Each of you are being called to teach this to others. They will listen to what you say. They will recognize it as the truth and the light. It is the way of God and the Light.

This Light will shine brightly. It will bring the people to listen and learn. It will then continue to grow in strength and numbers. It is time to fly free! Fly, Fly, Fly and be free!

Love and Light always!

                                                  Angels of God's Light and Love

Shine Bright!

ANGEL TALK / CHATTING WITH THE ANGELS

Angel Message: Dec. 17, 2002

"Our journey here is difficult. There is so much hatred and cold, cold hearts. This causes so much tension and will not allow the light to shine from one person to another.

As World Angels, it is your responsibility to unite and teach what is written. It is time for the world to hear and see what hatred can do to people and the world. When will the people on earth wake up and see the truth? Tell them it is time to wake up. Know that the color of skin, religion, and differences of the body do not matter. It is what is in the heart that matters.

When you connect the God spark inside each of you, the Light grows brighter. The people will awaken. They will start to see and feel the Christ within. It is time for all to awaken. Feel and see all that there is here on Earth for each and everyone who is here. Life is a blessing for all. It is a blessing from God to live a wonderful full life."

Angel Message: June 7, 2003

"We are calling louder to tell you it is time to pray. Pray for your world. Help is needed to shine the light brighter in this world. When the World Angels unite, many will follow once you start working towards this mission.

The task at hand is not an easy one, but a very necessary one.

SECTION FIVE: UNIVERSAL ANGEL MESSAGES

Many lives will be so affected by these events that are coming soon. It will be a chain of events. Too much for a human to exist with right now. So we just ask for people to Pray, Pray, and Pray.

Fly with us, we have been waiting, it has been way too long! Fly, fly, and fly!!! We are all one and always will be. Our mission is your mission. We need to work closer together to wake up the world.

It has had a wonderful start by others but it is time to turn the light on full force. Let the light begin to beam out. Share it with others. There are many blessings waiting for all of mankind!

We are celebrating here tonight for the world. Remember to just let go. Let go, let us help and allow the God force or spark to ignite. It will light your world with a fire so bright, nothing will be able to stop it.

Complete trust is all we are asking for now. We are asking you to start to become aware of us, and the energy that is here. Ask us for what you need. We ask you to have a deep and total trust. Keep gratitude in your heart. That is all that is needed. Prepare the way for the Celebration.

Love and Light,

Your Band of Angels

ANGEL TALK / CHATTING WITH THE ANGELS

This is one message I received one evening in 2004.

Hello Angels is there anything you would like for me to write about tonight?

They asked me to tell you this,

> "You can listen to us sing. You can become so overwhelmed with love, with an understanding of issues of the world. You will see these issues in a different light and begin living your life in a different way."

I received this next verse from the Angels at Christmas time on **December 2003**

The Angels signed it: "Angels of God's Light"

"Why is Christmas only celebrated one time a year?"

> "Christmas time brings about so much hustle and bustle. It becomes such a hectic time of year. Christmas is an event that should radiate love! Take time now to sit and meditate on the true meaning of Christmas. Bring this focus inside your heart. Allow the softness of this to spread throughout your body, mind and soul. Regardless of all the different opinions of what Christmas is about, or all of the different beliefs systems, the Holiday season should unite not divide. Celebrate all beliefs and take the truths from each and learn.

SECTION FIVE: UNIVERSAL ANGEL MESSAGES

> Then fill yourself completely with this true season of loving and giving. Giving of oneself and loving others is what this season is all about.
>
> This is the beginning of the New Year, not the ending of the old one. You build on all that you take from one year to the next. We say you will need to build the love, compassion and the generosity. You can only then take it into the next year and throughout your lives."

Angels of God's Light and Love   Dec. 2003

February 8, 2003

I asked tonight for the Angels to give me a message for the world. The following is what I was given.

> Pray, Pray, Pray for Peace. Send out the energy to all of the Leaders of every country. We watch as the pot boils. It is ready to boil over. Send energy and a radiant blue light to all of the soldiers. Surround them in God's Love. It is time to send the energy to all in the world.
>
> This is a time of great joy, it is an awakening but at the same time a tremendous sadness for so many.
>
> Change can sometimes be so sad, but will turn into much peace. So many changes for the world are soon to appear.
>
> Your Angels

ANGEL TALK / CHATTING WITH THE ANGELS

Jan. 10, 2004

This is another message I received one evening when I was listening to the Angels sing. What an awesome thing to cherish!

"The sound of an Angel brings us Peace, when their mighty voices ring out. They will bring Peace to all and the Universe in the wisp of a word.

Christine please tell others this message and keep it in your heart as well:

How you live your today will be your tomorrows.

Make the most of each new day to have only the greatest tomorrows!

Remember to keep your hearts full of happiness, love, and gratitude. Celebrate all good things. Then you will travel in the right direction."

From: The Angels of God's Light and Love

January 26, 2004

"Our Christine, the time has come now to put your mind in a direction so that things will come faster. Send the energy out and watch as situations occur and the miracles begin to happen.

SECTION FIVE: UNIVERSAL ANGEL MESSAGES

We are here and very excited to have you on our team, to help spread the word with us. Many more are needed. We are in our gathering phase and our spreading phase now.

Soon the word and light will become so bright that the energy shift will occur. It will be so magnificent! Most will not be able to ignore such a change on your planet earth.

Go now, pray and keep the Light Bright. "

Angels of God's Light

February 9, 2004

GOD

What a controversial word these days! All the following names make reference to God: Father God, Mother God, Father Mother God, Universal Energy, the Source, the Higher Power. I begin to wonder if we are even allowed to say God anymore.

I have become so aware of others and how they feel. You do not know whether to even say, "God bless you", when someone sneezes or coughs. It is such a small simple prayer, "God bless you." I do not know about anyone else, but I can sure use as many blessings as I can get!

This is what I hear the Angels teaching about tonight.

"How sad this world has become! Everyone tip toes around not knowing if it is okay to even mention this little three letter word. It seems to have taken on a magnificent power all of its own.

G.O.D.!

We tell you to hear us! This can stand for Grand, Omnipresent and Divine. That is kind of a nice thing we would think!

How sad all of this is!

OR...... Is it?

Since all of this controversy has occurred, it has actually raised the vibrations of the energy! Before all of this occurred, a lot of people took for granted the purpose of God."

I thought about what the Angels wrote and begin to write about it. I was given this message from the Angels:

"You just thought your rights to believe would always be there. You were taught prayers that sometimes were mindlessly recited. You talked somewhat about God and may have mentioned the word here and there. You even got to the point of using the small little prayer of "God bless you" without really thinking about it. Maybe everyone was getting all too comfortable in their own beliefs without being aware of others and what they believe.

SECTION FIVE: UNIVERSAL ANGEL MESSAGES

You now have all of the controversy facing you and the world. With all of the separation of church, state and the removal of God from different places and things. You have become awakened. People's emotions are stirring. This is the energy of an awakening. You are being told to wake up and pay attention. Do not take what you have now in your hearts for granted anymore.

Bring this emotion in and become aware of the God spark within yourself. Get a personal relationship with this energy. Then and only then can you materialize this. Let this spark take on a light. It becomes a beacon of light to shine out and touch others.

Everyone has the ability to manifest this light to shine and touch others. Does this mean go out and push your beliefs on others or condemn others for their beliefs? NO! Every one has a right to believe however they choose to believe. No one else should have the right to tell anyone how to believe.

This is why it is so important for each person, to develop a strong relationship with his or her God, no matter what you call this wonderful powerful, loving Energy!

That way when you are confronted, you will know your own strength and you can defend it. It becomes a part of your being. You will know and feel it to the very core of who you are.

When it becomes that much a part of your being, you will stand strong and not falter in your belief.

Take the time to stand out there. Join the other beams of light and help light up the world. Wonderful changes can and will occur when people join together as one.

Ask for guidance. The Angels will help. All you need to do is ask. In working with the preservation of beauty and harmony throughout the world, you all need to respect each other's beliefs, even if some are just totally opposite of yours. Respect each other. Let them grow in the direction they are going. You might be surprised one day to find they are not as different as you originally thought. They may still be so different, but the change you see is peace between the differences. Because it just does not matter anymore.

Now see where this will all lead, just because someone gave up trying to control how others believed.

"Controversy", being the idea that this has to be my way or no way

Vs

"Peace and contentment", it does not matter any longer, because we celebrate life and all of its differences.

We learn so much in life from all of the differences. If you can let go of being insulted or indignant of each other and in the way others believe, you will find inner peace, which will result in an Outer Peace as well.

SECTION FIVE: UNIVERSAL ANGEL MESSAGES

Now you wonder how I can do this. Once again you start with yourself. Work on what you can do to change your views. Begin your journey of walking with the Angels.

Once you start to feel this heaven within, you will find the opportunity arises to speak up and defend the right to be different. You will talk about how much you can learn from each other. Then start to watch the peace beginning to flow. You have created the beginning of a chain of light. A light so strong so powerful even the strongest storm will not be able to put it out.

Face this challenge. Step out, put your armor on and light the torch to be passed. Remember this is a great responsibility. I can tell you, each and every one of you is capable of accomplishing this challenge!"

3RD Assignment:

Prepare for the Angels and Let go of blocks

The following is how to prepare for the Angels and how to let go of what may be blocking your potential in life.

Take a few minutes to go inward to find something that is bothering you.

Feel it, then become aware of this energy. Watch the light start to glow around this situation, feeling or whatever you have chosen.

Now see the hands of God open. These hands are ready to take this from you, the whole thing, all which is involved. Get ready to hand it off. Turn it over and put it into God's hands.

Watch it leave.

Now take a deep breath and release it! All of it.

Suddenly the energy of Peace enters filling you with the most unimaginable feeling of peace. Do not think ahead or let your mind wonder about anything. Allow yourself to become this wonderful feeling of peace.

Now you are resonating at a higher level.

You are now prepared to ask for the Angel of Peace to enter.

3rd ASSIGNMENT: PREPARE FOR THE ANGELS AND LET GO

At this time ask for the Angels to help you carry this peace with you when you leave here. Incorporate this into your life.

You can still find that you have stumbled and backtracked every once in awhile. It is okay. You have now asked for this Angel of Peace. It is here to help you. You have felt it now. So you will find it hard to live without this emotion. You will want it to be with you in all things.

This is the Angel's mission in your life, to help you feel at peace in your heart, mind, body and soul. Feel this to the very depths of your being. Now we thank the Angels and believe this to be true.

Try to retain this feeling, the feeling you had when you held onto it. This will be easier each time you release and let go of all of the strings of attachments. This may take some time, depending on the situation. You my have to release it several times but the Angels are now helping the situation.

Which would you rather have? The feeling you had before this meditation that held you back and kept you down, or this feeling of peace and freedom?

Once you decide to find this great feeling of peace and contentment, you will be able to travel along this life in a new way.

Write about your experiences with your 3rd Assignment:

SECTION FIVE: UNIVERSAL ANGEL MESSAGES

Passion For Life

June 2006

Hello Angels, is there anything you would like me to write about tonight?

"Yes, there is so much we, on this side of life see. We see the lack of passion on your side of life. We see the lack of passion for living a life through God's eyes. The vision here is so different. We do not see the differences in the people who come here, such as the human beings there see. We see beauty in all humans, all souls. On this side it is all about beauty, peace and love for each other.

Your side was made as a mirror of our side of life. Your side was made to reflect our side of life. It really still does this very thing. Unfortunately, the humans who walk this time in life, just cannot for some reason, look into this mirror and see the reflection of beauty. They can not feel the love that is radiating to your side of life.

We ask that everyone take one day, just one day, to start to have Peace. Look at each other as the souls God created. Find the Peace and see the Beauty that each human possesses!

> Look again and see, because once you witness this, you cannot see things in reverse again. Open your eyes and see all the Beauty God has for Thee"

Angels of God's Wisdom and Beauty of Light!

June 16, 2008

This is an entry where I asked them, where do I take this book? What direction should I go? I asked the Angels to talk to me about writing. I know I need to write because the messages keep coming. I know you want others to look at people differently. You want us all to get along. You want us to look at each other and see the love that God poured into each one of us, not the hatred and differences. You have given me many messages that say the same thing only with different words.

A Troubled World

I asked them what they wanted to say about this topic.

The Angels say:

> "People still are not listening! This is why there is a need for this book. This is why you need to write to touch more and let them hear of the warnings. There are warnings that all is not well with this world. There is much trouble and it is not just the country of the United States, it is the whole world.

SECTION FIVE: UNIVERSAL ANGEL MESSAGES

Unless there are changes made throughout the world, there will be darkness, like no other. This darkness will not leave until the people of your world decide they can live together in the light.

The battles of religion, politics, and race need to be buried and allowed to die out, so that the light can shine. This is not meant to say, kill each other off, instead it is to say, help each other bring peace to the nations.

The tears fall here on our side. The tears fall in torrents of waterfalls for your world. We only have a short time to help. Then we must step back and allow your free will to take you down.

This is our warning. If you do not want the changes to come then you must hear and do something to change the world. Each person in this world can make the changes.

They can start with something small in their own lives. You can take a small amount of time each day, to do something nice for someone else. You can make a difference and this will make a change."

ANGEL TALK / CHATTING WITH THE ANGELS

I received this message about the time of the election of the President.

> This is an election year for the president of the United States. It gets very ugly and the Angels want us to: *"Pray, pray, pray!!!"*
>
> "They shout, "PRAY for the best outcome for your United States. We ask you to stand united and not divided. That is what elections do. They divide your world into little groups of people. That rips a tear in you so big, that it makes the world very weak and very vulnerable.
>
> When will everyone learn not to focus on the evil? Instead you need to focus on the good in the world?
>
> Find the good in each person that will make them the best candidates. We ask for these people to join together and put your country together. Do not keep it divided.
>
> We believe the saying is, "United we stand, divided we fall". Right now it looks like you are falling! Any country that fights amongst them will never stand strong."
>
> They say to tell all of you, "Once you start to unite together, then you will see the change that you so long for. The change will never come unless you join together and decide you want the good for all people!

SECTION FIVE: UNIVERSAL ANGEL MESSAGES

This is a message for the entire world not only the United States. In all countries, differences of opinion cause an upheaval. Differences cause a great strife in countries. We ask that these differences be put to rest. Come to an understanding that the only way out of all of this commotion is a peace of mind and peace of heart.

Come together in the world with Peace. Join the Light Beams that radiate to the earth plain. Join these beams together and unite them as one strong ray of light that is focused on each person to change them with a healing.

This healing force will be felt throughout the world. It will radiate through all mankind and all the earth."

*H*elp In Troubled Times

This next entry is included to give those people hope, who are feeling the energy of the world and who are feeling the extreme emotions of it all.

The Angels want to bring you peace and to let you know that they are working from their side to bring us the peace we all so deserve.

"Know that we are close for you to call upon. We are closer than you think! We stand beside you. We move in and we walk amongst all.

We touch your heart at the moment you think you cannot stand it any longer. We are there when you just do not know which way to turn.

When you are at your weakest moments, we are there to stand and hold you strong. Hold your head up high and know that you do make a difference. Know that you are showing others the light when you smile or when you cry along with them. Either way, you are doing for others.

Be prepared for the battle to get worse before it gets better. The battle is within so many. That is why you feel so lost. You do not know which way to turn and you are caught up in the whirlwind of emotions. You must let go and allow us to talk now.

Christine, take this time to put your hands together in prayer. Ask others to join you in this time of prayer. Prayer is all that can help. One little prayer each day and one little act of kindness will eventually save this planet called earth.

It is that simple and clear. Can each person take this time out to do just that one little simple exercise each day? Pay attention to those around you when you make your own changes.

The sky is blue and the hearts are cold. It is time to melt the hearts of many with love. Love really does make the world go round and round!"

SECTION FIVE: UNIVERSAL ANGEL MESSAGES

*G*roup Consciousness

This next message was given on the same night to those who are being called to create a group of like-minded people. They are being called to meet and work together to bring a balance to the energy of the world. I was shown this several years ago and we have been meeting once a month ever since.

> "Hang your head and bow your knees it is time to pray. Reach out to others, there are many there to help you with this mission.
>
> Your group, dear Christine must do the prayers for others. The work is great for the light of the world.
>
> Your mission with several groups is to shine the light for all to see.
>
> Group consciousness is not just for this side. We ask for you on your plane to start your groups of like-minded people. You can then put that consciousness to work for the good of all mankind. Put it out there, whatever your group needs. Put it out in the universe, then let us take it from there.
>
> As long as you put it out to us with a pure heart and soul, we can work with it from here. Keep the intention pure and very clear. We will see it for the light being it is.

You see that thoughts do become light energy and it is radar on our screens on this side. We pick up the transmission of energy. We will make it happen to bring it to usefulness and then back to you.

Each one in the group should become ready soon. Each person, we tell you once again, has a part in this action that is taking place.

Reach others and ask them to begin this action with you. Put people together to begin this form of work.

Small groups can meet. Then they will meet with the whole group to bring together the action that must take place. Bring it together we ask you soon. Bring it together we pray.

Send the beams of light out and ask it to find those who can help in a unique way. This is a commitment once again being asked for. Not all are up to the task at this time. People must rise to the occasion and bring this about to make the steady changes faster. Raise the vibrations and raise them faster. This must speed up quickly. Call out for help and we will send it on its way.

Sleep now dear one and write again soon. Each day now we ask you to come and speed up the writing. It is now that these words are needed.

SECTION FIVE: UNIVERSAL ANGEL MESSAGES

Now we ask that you tell others. First and foremost it is asked that you start the groups. We say thank you and God speed."

The Angels of God's light and love!

Sleep…………..Sleep……………Sleep………...sssssssssssslllll.

With this last message I am told we all need to work on getting together in groups of friends to sit together and pray. If we all stand strong in this world and work to raise the vibrations, we will stand victorious! So the Angels are saying that God wants us to stand strong and unite so we can bring peace to all nations.

June 20, 2008

The Shift That Happens

This morning is the Summer Solstice.

While I am sitting and eating my breakfast I began to hear the air sing.

Then I heard these words:

"We are here today to teach another world lesson. It is our wish that God's people listen to these words and take them to heart.

The things that happen in this world are not caused by God or by this so-called being that everyone calls, Satan.

People give this energy a name of Satan and people say all of the time that this Satan caused this and that. They even give credit to this energy for people's death. People have given this energy a human form, a human presence and this gives it the power to begin to take shape in this world. People are saying that this Satan has the power to punish different people for their ways of life or beliefs.

We the Angels deliver this message today to wake the people of the world up with this lesson. We are here to tell you the more you keep giving this a negative energy, in the multitude it is given, you can sit back and watch how much farther God moves from the world. God is being pushed out of this world with the hatred and negativity that is being projected out into the world.

The shifts that happen in this world are caused by all of the righteous beliefs, negative thoughts and words, created by the human beings of all religions and races. All of mankind is responsible for creating this mess in the world.

SECTION FIVE: UNIVERSAL ANGEL MESSAGES

God created the most beautiful world and set it all in motion. It was balanced, peaceful and glorious. Nature ruled the world. When God decided to share it all, things began to change. God is glorious and wondrous. He gave you free will to change this world, in whatever way you needed to make it work for you. God stood back and gave you freedom. He only asked that you love one another as much as he loves each of you. He then set it up for all of His people to roam this great planet and multiply.

Natural Law was at work for all of mankind. This means that whatever you do has a side effect, good, bad or indifferent. If you put out negativity you create it around you and for others. You put out love and it will always flow back to you."

God's Energy in Motion

"You are not a puppet on a string! There is no great puppeteer in the sky called, "God", controlling you. You are free to come and go at will. You are free to do whatever you have the will to do. Remember though, there are Laws in motion that will respond to the actions you take.

We have a few lessons for you to learn. We would like to share them with each of you at this time.

Call God up sometime. Sit right down and take time out to listen.

God is an energy that is full of light, love and power to do all things. Call on this energy to fill you to the very brim and allow it to overflow. When you do this, look around you and feel the love that fills you.

Begin to feel this love and begin to see all mankind. Begin to feel the love for all of this mankind and for all creation. Feel this without prejudice or resentment from a loving heart center. This is God and God's word.

If at this time you feel anything else but peace and love for this world and your fellow person, this is from the human form that you are in at this time. This other feeling is not from God.

Blessings everyone on earth and all creations. We sing joyful music for all to hear!

Believe this! Feel this love and all else is only an illusion. It is created by you from the human part of your world."

SECTION FIVE: UNIVERSAL ANGEL MESSAGES

Kind and Gentle Reminders

"Everyone is so busy trying to change the world and the people in it. They want things or people to fit their mold of belief, instead of living a simple life and enjoying all creation. You are so busy working until all hours of the night and rushing here and there. When was the last time you took time to stop, look around, and enjoy your surroundings?

We are not telling you not to work nor to not do the things that you enjoy. It is when you are so consumed with making more and more money, just so you can have more or bigger and better, that is when you become unbalanced.

Working is needed. Money is needed for this lifetime, we understand. We ask you, when the last time you actually stopped to help someone else or at least helped someone else without thinking? You may ask, "How can I take time out of my busy life to sit and talk to the person?" If you would take the time, you might find the person who really could have used your help in their life.

How often have you gotten up from your sleep, only to realize that it has been weeks or even years since you talked to someone you really care about, because you are so overwhelmed with life?

Think about these things that have all been mentioned this day. Think where you could make some changes and watch as your world begins to heal, and the people of your world will begin to heal with it. Changes will occur! Light will shine again!

These words are not reprimands. They are kind and gentle reminders to wake up now, right now. Take time to live your life. Do not let life live around you, without you being a participant!"

Angels of God's Divine Promises

Trapped in Life

July 5, 2008   1:38 AM

Happy 4th of July here in the USA! I tried to lie down to sleep a little while ago, only to be brought back to the computer to write a message from the Angels. They were talking to me about feeling trapped in our lives. They were making comments to me about this topic of not moving forward in life. This is the message they gave me to share, when we just stand still, eventhough we can see that it is time to move forward in life.

SECTION FIVE: UNIVERSAL ANGEL MESSAGES

"Christine dear,

This is what happens to those who choose to stand still. We will give you an example of what it is like from our viewpoint. We will then give you a choice at the end.

You are standing in the bottom of a dry well with very smooth sides all around and no way out. Suddenly you start to notice that the well is leaking water. It is slowly starting to come in the sides and running down around your feet. The water begins to rise. You find that you are just standing there, frozen in time. You can not seem to breathe.

There is a feeling of panic in life. Things start to come in around you. It makes you feel frozen in space and time.

Now here is one choice. Do you just stand there, not trying to move around at all? Do you let the water come up around you, to just drown in life?

Imagine being frozen in time with all of this stuff all up around you. It starts to cover you from head to toe. You are not able to pull yourself up and out of the water.

Water represents your emotions here in this story.

How much of your time are you willing to waste here in this life doing just that? Standing still and not moving.

Here is another choice. You see that you are standing in water. You may hesitate just a little bit longer than you should, so the water starts to come up around you.

You start to try to figure it out, but you just can not see past where you are. Then suddenly, you feel the desire to start to paddle your legs. You find you are treading this water and staying a float.

You are at least keeping your head above the water but you are getting very tired, very quickly. You are not sure that you can keep treading for very much longer.

This is where just a little bit of help could come in handy. This is where you say, I am really very exhausted now and I know I need help. I am not sure where the help will come from, but I have faith that I can find it somewhere.

You can call out to see if anyone is passing by and will come to help you.

You have people around that can help you sometimes make sense of things in life.

If no one comes along to help, you can just float a bit longer without treading to take a break. As the water keeps filling the well, allow us, the Angels to float along with you.

SECTION FIVE: UNIVERSAL ANGEL MESSAGES

Soon you will find that you can reach the top end of the well. You can then pull yourself up and out.

Begin to look around and see how you came to be at the bottom of that well. Look for a way that will help you not to get yourself at that point in life, you end up at the bottom of the well again.

You can do this, by making the changes that are needed in your life to bring you back on the path of life, with the least resistance.

So you see, you always have a choice on how you will handle situations in life.

You can let your emotions run away with the situations in life. This will keep you frozen in the unhealthy environments around you. Or you can choose to find the help you need to get through the difficult times.

We do suggest that you find the help, to move forward past these situations, and find the best path for you at that time. If you do it the way of least resistance then you will find that you come out on the other side with more learned and less exhaustion.

That is the lesson for this evening about being trapped in life. We hope you will find that you do have the ability within yourselves to move along from here with less bumpy roads."

Blessing and Light with God's blessings from above!

Fate, Karma and Free Will

July 6, 2008 11:05 AM

I was just thinking about the sermon I was going to do tonight about freedom. A conversation I had this week came into my mind about what the difference between fate, karma and free will were and I heard this answer.

> "Fate is a thing that is meant to happen. Fate and Karma are destination points in life. Karma is what you are working through in life to get to the end point.
>
> Free will enters into the picture because that is the vehicle we use to get to the end point. It is how we get to the different destination points. We make the decisions through life based on the circumstances at the time. That is how we work our way through life to learn what we needed to learn or experience in Fate and Karma.
>
> Our life is a lesson. How we learn that lesson is up to us. Whatever road we take, will teach us that lesson in a different way. How you learn or if you learn that lesson at all, will determine if you will need to learn it again and again and again.

SECTION FIVE: UNIVERSAL ANGEL MESSAGES

So, try through out your lifetime, to only have to learn things once. Then it will not be so hard to grasp the life lesson you needed to experience.

Sometimes the lesson comes on a little lighter, but then you do not listen. Or you may not see what was being shown. The opportunity to learn it will arise again at some point in your life.

The fate and karma end of it dictates that you must learn this in this lifetime. If you do not, then the opportunity will come again to give you that chance to find the answer or at least for you to have that experience in life.

We work with you during these times to help you grow. God has asked us to except this job so that we can help direct you along the way. We will then hold you up during the life experiences.

We will dance with you as you celebrate your education! God wants the best for everyone in life! We are here to help make that a possibility.

This is our talk today on Fate, Karma and Free will. It is all just a fact of life.

The Angels of God's Love and Light!

Wake Up and Do God's Work

That same night just a little later I heard this next message. It is one of my personal messages, but I am told to enter it in the book. This is so the others who are hearing the call of the Angels, will know that is time to wake up and do God's work. The Angels do not want you to feel so alone:

"Good Morning Dear One,

> Live your life today. Do not waste a single moment looking back in time. Only look ahead and plan what you will want to see in your future. Write an outline of what you want to have and what you want to do. Allow us to help you get there. Make your destination a great one. We are here to assist you in this life. Utilize our help. Make your decisions, based upon what you have learned throughout life.
>
> You now know your direction or at least we hope that it is clear by now. You know your destination is doing God's work. That is where we ask you to be. It is all about working on lighting the world on fire, to brighten up the world from the darkness that is here. Begin lighting the world on fire, with the Light of God's Love and Light.

SECTION FIVE: UNIVERSAL ANGEL MESSAGES

The warm glow will ignite and spread throughout all nations. The love will grow so bright that it will warm God's whole being. God's energy is what you will utilize throughout this work.

You will not go this path alone. We have called others. People know it is time to speed this process up and move forward starting today.

So begin today, with writing your life plan down. We will help you with this plan. Know that you will be helping many along the way, to see the world in a different light.

Our work with God will change nations.

Begin to work hard with dedication and determination. Begin to see the path light up for your eyes and ears to understand our words today.

The Angels Love and Light!

Freedom

July 7, 2008   1:32 AM

Dear Angels what would you like to talk with us tonight about?

"Dear ones we would like to intercede at this point and talk to this nation about Freedom. We will talk about your Freedom to choose your way and the Freedom to treat others in whatever way you choose. This Freedom that everyone does celebrate in the USA is a freedom that others will one day see the need for. We speak tonight about a freedom to be your self and not be ridiculed for doing so. This will be one way for others to incorporate free will into their lives.

Be very careful how you interpret freedom though. Freedom does not mean that you can inflict your opinions and views onto others through force. It does not mean that you can do whatever you want to others to harm them in any way.

God gave all of you freedom through choice so that you could find your way in life. So you could find a way to live in harmony together. We seem to talk about this topic much. We know we do but sometimes we wonder who is listening.

SECTION FIVE: UNIVERSAL ANGEL MESSAGES

We talk about it in different ways to try to get the point across for the humans in this world to all understand.

Emotions?

We will talk tonight about another topic. This topic is about emotions. Feelings of compassion, are a great thing to carry with you.

Emotions are things that can get carried away by some. Others will never show it to anyone else for fear they will get hurt. What a wild ride this emotion is.

What was our God thinking by creating such things as emotions?

Well, if you had no emotions you could never appreciate anything, love anyone or anything. You would never feel anything good, bad or indifferent. We will try to figure out what good emotions are for you, as a human and let you know. It is hard sometimes for us because we have a certain way we look at things. Sometimes it can be a very narrow pont of view.

We can not always tell the side - tracked areas of life. We can mostly see the straight and narrow. Emotions are things that we do not always have.

We feel the energy from your earth. This does teach us to understand some of what you do go through on your earth plane.

We just can not sit and not accomplish things because of the energy we get a feeling for, from all of the humans. We do however care deeply for each individual, otherwise how would we know how to interact with you?

Sometimes we do hear people say Angels have no emotions. They have misunderstood something here. We do not have emotions such as you as humans have. They are very different, because we do not react to them in the same manner as you. We do however understand them.

We can sit and hold you when you cry. We will carry you along the way when you need to be carried. We can run with you in the field of flowers and sing a beautiful song. We can enjoy life right along with you. It is an amazing understanding that God has granted us, so that we may interact more appropriately with the human beings that we are to help throughout this lifetime.

The Guardian Angels will have more reaction to your emotions than the Hierarchy will. Their jobs are much more powerful than other angels.

SECTION FIVE: UNIVERSAL ANGEL MESSAGES

Now we do hope that this information will be useful for those interested in how we interact with you on a personal level.

Let this be the end of this lesson for now. Come again and sit with us soon."

4th Assignment: A Release Technique

1. Begin by practicing being honest with yourself. Look at yourself and feel all that is there.

2. Write your list of things you are not happy with. Then write the things you are happy with. Then look at your list of unhappy or discontent items and honestly evaluate them to see how important each thing is.

3. Then determine what you can change and make better. The things you cannot change, meditate on and ask for a way to accept them. Then you can begin to find peace in your heart over them.

4. Now look at your list and see the things you are happy with and determine how important they are. Can you make any of these things even better? How do these positive things help you to be better? How can they help others?

> "We the Angels of God, hear your prayers and work to help you find that peace.
>
> We ask that you trust us. Know that we hear you. Then accept that we have heard you. Believe that we help you create the changes inside and outside yourselves."

I then asked the Angels about forgiveness because they had mentioned it several times today.

4th: ASSIGNMENT: A RELEASE TECHNIQUE

5. Letting go and releasing things from the past is not always an easy task. By starting inside yourself and forgiving yourself for thing you have done is another key to finding Peace in your heart. Once you forgive yourself, you can release the emotions you have, whenever you let someone down or do something you would regret later.

6. Then you begin to go through your life and write the names of anyone you can remember that in some way hurt you or did something that you took offense to.

7. Take each name on your list and say out loud or to yourself:

> a) You are a Child of God; I release the feelings surrounding our conflict and send back these emotions to God to heal.
>
> b) I now send light, love and peace of heart back to you.
>
> c) Rest now and feel the pleasure of peace in your heart center.
> d) Become aware and watch the peacefulness grow! It will start to spread all around and continue to grow.
>
> e) Here and now is the time to allow the peace to enter your heart and grow outward into your every day life.
>
> f) Begin to project it outwards, watch as it swirls around with all of the lights of colors. It grows brighter and brighter.
>
> g) Let it go and let the feelings in.

The Angels end this technique with these thoughts:

> "Your thoughts are growing stronger and coming to life quickly, so yes it is moving faster and faster. The energy is flowing fast and furious. You will not miss the boat. It can not sail without you.
>
> Come aboard and enjoy the ride.
>
> As you do this release technique, you will start to notice how your heart and mind change towards these incidents. Little by little you will notice a healing taking place within yourself.
>
> Sending positive back to the person will also help them as well as release you from the negative hold, bitterness and resentment a painful heart can have on you."

Write your experiences in your journal from the 4th Assignment.

SECTION FIVE: UNIVERSAL ANGEL MESSAGES

Calling The World Angels

July 10, 2002

Dear Angels what message do you have for me tonight?

"Heavenly beings, heavenly beings are all around,

some flying, some walking,

and some just sitting still and watching.

Heavenly beings, alive and well,

here to stay for eternity.

Stop and see.

Be still and listen.

When you ask you will see and hear.

We are here now to stay."

Olivetta

ANGEL TALK / CHATTING WITH THE ANGELS

"Christine, dear child of God, The breath of life was blown into your body. When it was, your heart started to beat. Your blood flowed. Your lungs and brain started working. As you grow everything continues to work together. Remember to value life. Keep healthy, sleep well, drink your water, play in the water and take care of Mother Earth.

Prepare yourself now for what is to come.

We are here helping you to grow and mature. The teachings have begun and will continue to grow.

Sleep dear child, Sleep now!"

Angels of Light

July 24, 2002

"Angels, Angels, Angels, all around. We are always around helping and working. Please be aware. Give credit to your Heavenly Father, Mother/Father God is always here. Ready to help at all times. Place your life in the Energy of God. Things will work out and be just fine. Hang in there! Things will be just fine!

Your Angels of God's Light!

SECTION FIVE: UNIVERSAL ANGEL MESSAGES

August 2, 2002

I hear a song start singing again, "Angels, Angels, Angels, Angels." It is like a chant in many different harmonies.

"Christine our sweet child, do not worry! The jobs will be done! You keep moving forward. There are many that need to hear our words. We will fill the void! Allow this to flow. Thank you for letting this flow and the Light of God to shine. Bring about the Peace and Harmony!

The tiredness will cease and you will once again be filled with the joy of life! We will fill you totally with the breath of God's love!

We want you to see and feel us! Be aware! Take the time to stand with us! Be around us we will float you on the way. Time is at hand to shine.

This work needs the leaders! World Angels unite! Stand strong! Believe and teach. Allow the followers to join up and stand tall! Connect with others and learn all that you can. People recognize this as the truth and the light. It is the way of God, the Light. It is growing and growing Always!

Time to fly!   Love and light,

      Angels of God's Light and Love!!!

Shine Bright!!

I included this message so others can see that the Angels know that we want to understand things in this world. They want us to know they are willing to work with us in all areas of our life. They ask for the leaders to come forth and help with this work.

I want to encourage those who have had similar experience to step up at this time to listen and learn. Then come out and teach others as we join together to make the changes necessary for this world to grow in God's love and light!

Each person that is reading this book is being called to do God's work in some way. You did not just pick this book by accident.

You have felt the longing or you have been having the urge to learn more about what talking with the Angels is all about. You want to know why the Angels are working amongst us all so much more.

So now you might ask, "What and where do I go from here?" You might just begin to see people differently and just see how they need your help.

It could come to you in the way of feeling different inside or just knowing that something needs to be accomplished. There could be a nagging feeling inside you to do something different and not knowing exactly what that might be.

There can be other sign. Just start to pay attention. The Angels are calling you for the purpose of helping others.

SECTION FIVE: UNIVERSAL ANGEL MESSAGES

You are being called to stand up to make changes in your own life to bring yourself in alignment with the God energy.

We are asked to make our commitment now. This commitment to being a soldier for God does not mean that you go out and fight battles of war. It is bringing about the state of Peace and well being amongst those around you.

Some are called to go out and work in the world. Others are being called to work amongst the people in their lives by setting examples.

I remember when I was asked to make this commitment. I was told by the Angels, this was a very great privilege and would make major changes in my life. It did make major changes.

Sometimes I felt I had adjusted too quickly, and others I fought. The ones I fought are the ones that took a bit longer to accomplish.

I did not know at the time I was fighting it. It was only later when looking back I could understand what happened with it all.

My request came **Sept. 4, 2003** in one of the Angel messages. I had been asked before this, but did not understand what it meant. In this meditation I received more of an idea:

"Christine, Christine." I heard this several times just a very soft whisper in the wind.

"We wait for your meeting! Remember the time has come for your commitment. Think and pray about it once the decision is made. Times will be so different. Things are in motion. It is time for your work to begin. Let us know soon.

Commitment is important. We understand if you walk away. If you choose to say yes to us, you will start to see the change in the physical.

We love you and can not wait to get started. Remember that this is a serious request. This is not just your imagination. This is a request to work for God.

Go now and sleep. Get more rest for now, because the time is near. Rest will be less and less, but refreshment will always be there as well."

Love

The Angels of God - the Warriors of God in the Temple

Sept. 7, 2003

I had prayed about this message. I have talked to one of my friends, named David, who I had talked to before about this type of message. He had gotten some messages about this also. He had a feeling about it and we were meeting today.

SECTION FIVE: UNIVERSAL ANGEL MESSAGES

We talked with our spouses. We all agreed that we needed to say yes to the request. We got together this evening, went into meditation and the following is what transpired.

When we went into meditation, we were taken very close to the entrance to the Angels. We were only allowed so far and were stopped. We were then greeted by a group of Angels. We were asked what our decision was. We both told them we came to accept the work they had asked us to do. They had a book for us to sign and so we did. Then immediately after we signed our name, our full names appeared in bold print glistening in the book. We were then presented with armor, the whole outfit. We were told this would prepare us for the battle that lay ahead of us.

Joan of Arch was there and told us she would be of help. There was a sister who appeared. She told us she would be helping us learn the Spiritual answers. She told us her name was Anna.

When we looked around, we saw that many Angels and our guides had surrounded us. We were shown that we would be doing many healings and teachings with the lesson we would be taught.

We were taken on a path with the Angels. They said they would all be there with us on this road to help us. We were told we would know what to do or say when the time comes.

We then felt things begin to close down. We then realized it was time to leave. Then we saw a brilliant light coming towards us. We saw four Angels standing right in front of us with full armor.

There were other Angels standing by with instructions, to tell us about who these four Angels were. We were given instructions on what each of them would be helping us with as we moved forward with this commitment.

> "**Archangel Michael,** who is strong, has a booming voice and is very, very big in stature. He had been calling to me all week. He told us that he is the one to bring us the strength to do this work and bring us the words to use.
>
> **Archangel Gabrielle**, who is milder but could have a heavy hand if he needed one. He says that he comes to be the one who does the healing and smoothing the road ahead for us.
>
> **Archangel Uriel**, who is very strong also, but not as bold, more gentle handed. He says that he will help with the writing and teaching of the lessons.
>
> **Archangel Raphael**, the patient, loving and gentler Angel, full of song, he says he will teach us to relax into our work so we understand and love our journey."

SECTION FIVE: UNIVERSAL ANGEL MESSAGES

They then told us,

> "The deed that was asked of you was complete. Now the time has come to begin your journey. Plan and prepare. Go and be ready.
>
> Get your schedules together and plan what you need to do to prepare. Take this time to meditate on the next steps to take. We will tell you each step, as you go. This way it will not overwhelm you. You will succeed at this mission.
>
> Prepare yourself physically. Start daily walks. Drink more water, and eat fresh foods more often. Cleanse your bodies with fresh water daily. Walk 10-15 minutes a day to start, stretch then walk. This will help to clear your minds. You will then be ready for your work.
>
> This is your assignment until your next meeting with us. Go now. Rest and sleep. We will be working with you as you sleep.
>
> Your Angels, Love Sweet Love

Meditation #6: Expanding Your Consciousness

Would you like to experience this connection with the Divine energy of the Light?

We will begin with a very simple meditation.

This meditation was given to me one evening, so that I could teach people how to expand their consciousness and to become more aware of things around them. During the meditation, imagine the Angels talking to you and directing you on what to do.

1. Settle into your seat and find something in the room that you can focus on.

2. As you spend a few minutes looking at this object, begin to breathe in through your nose. Expanding the diaphragm as you breathe in to the count of eight. Hold for a count of eight, and then breathe out through your mouth to the count of eight. (Do this three times)

3. Allow your focus to gently float away from the object you have been focused on. Allow your eyes to slowly close.

4. Begin by saying the word OHM three times. This is done in a slow chant.

MEDITATION #6: EXPANDING YOUR CONSCIOUSNESS

As you begin to move forward, the Angels will take you off to the outer worlds that co-exist with our Universe.

Fly with us and let us take you beyond your reasoning! Go into the unknown and find a better place to live.

Leave your body behind. Leave your mind behind. You no longer need this entity. Gently floating, floating away.

Look around and see that you are in a new form. This is your light being….. Your divine being… Your state of consciousness of being all that is.

You are now only the energy, you need to survive in this experience.

You have now merged with all that is.

Take this time to float along and experience the Supreme Being you are.

***************** Time out meditation

If you can now accept this new life, you will experience a new awakening. It will begin slowly at first. Then escalate to a speed immeasurable in this world.

We understand you have a craving for more. This is the beginning of finding the more that you thirst for, everyday.

It is time to come back to this room. Do not leave your light behind. Come back with this torch of light that you will now carry with you for eternity.

This energy light will fill you and feed you, with all that you need. Use this light each day to bring about the newness in life.

You have had the experience of the feeling of being one with the God force. So from this day forward you have the experience of being one with the Universe.

Be careful how you use it. You must only use this for the empowering of yourself and others, to become one and co-exist in harmony in this world."

MEDITATION #6: EXPANDING YOUR CONSCIOUSNESS

Working With Your Creative Angels

SECTION SIX

SECTION SIX: WORKING WITH YOUR CREATIVE ANGELS

"Dream"

"Dream on dear children, dream of all there is in life.

Dream of the wonders of life the wonders from God.

These are the gifts bestowed upon you.

God has asked us to intervene and show you how wonderful life really is.

This life is a dream. The reality is that all is one with God.

Look at your life and dream of the many blessings coming your way over this lifetime.

Dream Big, Dream Beautiful, Dream into reality the wonders of life.

God Bless!"

Olivetta   Dec. 1, 2009

INTRODUCTION TO THE CREATIVE ANGELS

When you work with the Angels they love to share their gifts with you. When this happens you will begin to be blessed with many creative gifts over time. You can hear a song playing in your head that you feel inspired to sing or the words of a poem unfolding from your pen.

There are many forms of art that can happen such as; the ability to pick up a drawing pencil, crayon, chalk or paint and create the most wonderful Angel Art, although you really were never able to draw before. You find that you are drawn to stop by a bead shop and begin to pick through beads of all colors. You find you want to learn to wrap them with wire. You end up with a magnificent piece of Angel jewelry. There are many other forms of art and talents that remain to be discovered. Come and play with the Angels and together see what you can create!

SECTION SIX: WORKING WITH YOUR CREATIVE ANGELS

I have found that I have an Angel who signs the name, "Madrina" to most of the poetry that I have written as it comes to me. There is the Angel Art which comes through several Angels who love to draw the energy of the Angels. Olivetta is one of these Angels. I now notice that this Angel is doing some of the poetry also.

I am noticing, when I put together a necklace, sometimes the beads that I am wrapping with wire turn out looking like an Angel. This also happens when I am designing stained glass pieces out of the odd pieces of glass. I start to put it together and it comes out looking like an Angel.

It is always so much fun to see the finished product. Because with all of these gifts, I never really know what I am going to do with a piece of glass or a bead and wire or even with a colored pencil and a piece of paper, until it is all finished. I get the feeling that it is finished, then you look at it, there it is a finished piece of Art and it looks like an Angel.

You are inspired to continue exploring the vast array of things that you can accomplish with the influences of God's Angels. They are only encouraging you to use your natural God given abilities in life. Enjoy the exploration process to see what else you can create!

People ask me all the time, "How are you able to work with the Angels in this fashion?" I asked the Angels this question myself because, for a long time I was not sure how it all happened.

The answer to this question is very simple actually. They basically told me because I have asked for their help!

I am now sharing how these gifts have come to me. Here is a list of gifts I feel I have received over the past few years. There are other gifts I have heard that other people have received.

I have experienced the Angel writing, messages, Art, Poetry, jewelry making and Healing with the Angels.

Others have written music and put words to it, to come up with very inspirational music.

I have said this before. There are many more gifts still yet to be experienced, so please do not limit your potential to only those listed here!

SECTION SIX: WORKING WITH YOUR CREATIVE ANGELS

ANGEL POETRY

The angels sometimes love to talk to us in rhymes. In this section I am sharing the gift of writing the words of the Angels in a different format of Poetry. I have added to this section some of the poetry that I have received from Madrina my Poetry Angel. I have found over the years, I have heard from other Angels who love to write Poetry with me. There are two more that I know of at this time Olivetta and Hakiel

I was writing one night and these poems just started to flow. I heard the Angels say:

"Flows just like the river over time. See how that happens!"

It is so much fun. You start to write what is coming into your head. Sometimes you think to yourself this makes no sense. You try to go back over it to make some changes and find you can not change it. Before you know it, the poem or song is written and done. Then you go back over it just for your own curiosity, you read it and think, "Hey that sounds pretty good!"

You just keep it the way it comes into your mind. Do not change anything unless you first ask the Angel who is reciting the words to you.

ANGEL TALK / CHATTING WITH THE ANGELS

If there are any changes or additions to what was said it will turn out very interesting. The words are very blessed with much love and wisdom.

Sometimes I think it sounds like the way Jesus would have spoken while he lived in this world. He told stories or parables many times throughout his life.

The Angels told me,

"This was so people could think about what was being said, and begin to concentrate on it until they got the message that was meant for them."

This is what the Angels told me, is the purpose of these poems.

"These words are for you to read over and over again. You will get your message and healing from the words that fill your heart with the love that is being sent to you from God."

I have jotted some of these down throughout the book for your enjoyment.

SECTION SIX: WORKING WITH YOUR CREATIVE ANGELS

"FINDING PEACE"

Keeping your inner Joy alive, allows you to find the Peace

buried inside your heart.

Bringing this inner Joy outside your body, allows this Peace to

flow, from your heart to others.

This then brings Joy to each person they come in contact

with, bringing about a tidal wave of Love,

which in turn brings about Peace.

Without Joy and Love there is no Peace.

So bring out that Joy and let it grow into Love

which then creates Peace.

"Madrina"   Dec. 2003

(Written as given from an Angel who calls herself Madrina)

"JOY"

What is Joy? Where is Joy? How do we find it?

JOY….. such a simple word.

Only 3 letters J   O   Y

JOY

Embrace JOY and feel it.

Bring it deep inside your heart and live it.

Shout about JOY and share it with others.

Joy what is it? Where is it?

Is it an emotion or a sensation?

OR

Is it just there?

Can we find JOY?

SECTION SIX: WORKING WITH YOUR CREATIVE ANGELS

If we did what would you do with it?

JOY… how simple it is.

Feel it bring a smile to your face,

a glint of sparkle to your eyes

and a warmth to your heart.

Joy… live with it, cherish it!

Plain and simple it is JOY!

Madrina   Jan. 21, 2004

"Merrily, Merrily We Sing a Song!"

Merrily, Merrily we sing the song,

We sing the song of God....

Merrily, merrily we speak the words of God,

Joyfully, Joyfully we watch as you grow.

We help to shine, we help to shine

God's love and light.

Sing his song and speak his words

see all the glory, see it glow, all around.

        Madrina   Jan. 3, 2006

SECTION SIX: WORKING WITH YOUR CREATIVE ANGELS

June 25, 2008

Madrina, can you speak with me this evening?

"A Place of Love"

Join with me now to fly ever so high,

join with me now to take flight to above.

Flying so high into the silence above,

to take you to the place which is the place of love.

Hanging in space just hanging around,

To fill you with love from all that is found.

Peace inside and smiles all around,

To take you to the place that is off the ground.

Know that you can understand all that is,

by just finding the peace, which is promised to all a bound.

Tuesday April 7, 2001

Who's There?

"Who's There?" Who's There?

Where are you? What are you doing?

Where are you going?

Listen, Listen! Be still and listen.

Whisper, Whisper, Silently Whisper.

Hear us now? Hear us now?

Sit quietly and listen, now you hear us.

Follow us.

We will guide you along the way

Listen quietly, be still and follow

Who's there? Who's there?

SECTION SIX: WORKING WITH YOUR CREATIVE ANGELS

March 7, 2001

"Is Now The Time?"

Is now the time? Is now the time?

Is there anyone here, who cares?

Who will hear the messages I'm to give?

Is now the time? What's wrong with now?

Do we have any other time but now?

Take time out and focus in. Open wide without fear.

I am here. I bring with me lots of friends!

Love, Friendship, Comfort, Peace and Joy!

Just to name a few. Do you want to hear my words?

Do you want to feel my Peace, Joy and Love?

Do you have the time to let me be your friend?

Is now the Time?

Angel Message by Hakiel

MORE FROM MY NOTEBOOKS

FROM 2002 – 2004

Another Gift from the Angels

CROSSOVER EXPERIENCES

I was working with the Angels one spring evening in the year 1997 when the Angels asked me to follow them in my prayers. I was taken to a cool dark and damp place. I looked around for a bit. I asked, "Where am I? What are we doing here?" I heard an Angel tell me, "Wait, watch and listen."

I stopped walking and started to get my site more focused to the darkness. I then became aware of a very quiet crying. I could hear someone making some sniffling noises. I felt I needed to walk a little bit towards the crying sounds. It sounded like a child crying. I just needed to get to where this was coming from.

I suddenly became aware of a very young girl sitting on the ground. She had her head down on her knees and was all curled up in a ball. She was so sweet that I just had to go to her and see if I could help her. I became aware that we were in a sewer or drainage area.

SECTION SIX: WORKING WITH YOUR CREATIVE ANGELS

I then came close enough to touch this little girl. I wanted to let her know I was there so I would not scare her. I called very quietly to her and asked if I could help her.

She raised her little head and her big brown eyes looked up at me. She seemed surprised that I was there to help her. I told her that I would help her find her home. She started to cry even harder and told me she could not go home. I then asked her why? She said that she had been bad because she got lost and could not find her way home. She was afraid to return home. I then said that she could go home if she wanted to and she would be just fine.

The Angel then returned and looked at us both. I could see this Angel, but I could tell the little girl could not see it. I was told I needed to leave now, but I did not want to because I just wanted to help this little girl. I asked the Angel to at least let me get a blanket and a sandwich for the little one. I watched as the Angel covered her up and the little one ate. I was told she would be fine. I told the girl that the Angels would watch over her for a little while and I would be back soon.

Later that night, I was brought back to the little girl and then I could see she was not alive in this world. I was being shown that I needed to help her find her way to God's home. The place where she would be safe for eternity.

I was given a very beautiful white dress to put on this sweet little child. She was excited to put on such a nice dress.

I walked up to her and told her we needed to go for a walk. She cried out that she was afraid. I told her, "To just take my hand, I will lift you up and carry you along the way."

I wiped her tears away and held her close to me. I walked for just a bit. We saw the most brilliant light coming from deep in the tunnel that was so dark just a minute ago. This scared her a bit and she hid her face on my shoulder. I continued this journey for a bit and suddenly I felt like I was floating along. I noticed my feet were no longer on the ground. We were being lifted up into the air.

I told her to look at the beautiful light. She lifted her head, looked at the light and asked what it was. I told her it was the Angels and explained to her they were coming to take her to a wonderful play land. Then I told her that she would be safe and never be hurt again. She grew more excited about what was ahead and continued to gaze into the light.

A hand made of brilliant white light reached through the light toward us. A voice then sounded from the light and was asking her to take this hand. She did not want to and wanted me to do it instead. We floated a bit farther and we could feel the calming of the energy around us. We could make out figures ahead of us. They were just figures of light. They grew in numbers as we came closer. Suddenly, the child began to float and became very light. She looked at me and smiled. What a beautiful smile she had. Her eyes lit up and she said she was so happy.

SECTION SIX: WORKING WITH YOUR CREATIVE ANGELS

I told her it was okay for her to go. She looked at me a little bit and said she wanted me to come along. I had to tell her this was all the farther I would be allowed to go at this time.

We both turned around to see the most awesome sight of an Angel of Light that was all light energy. This energy brought so much peace and so much warmth that we could not refuse the offer to fly towards this light energy. This sweet little figure of a girl began to glow. She looked around and told me she was okay now. I said yes you are. She turned, looked at me again and kissed me on the cheek. Then she touched my face with her little hands. She then turned and floated off as she waved goodbye.

Once she was gone through the mist of the light, the area I was in became a wonderful liquid light. It surrounded me and filled me with such a warm feeling of inner peace and divine love! I could hardly handle the emotion that I felt well up inside me.

An Angel of Light came to me and thanked me for doing God's work with the Angels. This Angel told me that I was being called to continue doing this type of work. I was told that one of my titles would be a Worker of the Light. I would be shown the souls that needed help with their journey's home. I said, I really did not know what to do or how to do this because I had never heard of such a thing before.

The Angel told me they would teach me as we worked together to accomplish this mission.

Over the years I have done just that. I have also taught others to do this work. We now have a group that meets once a month, just for the purpose of helping the souls of those who do not understand what is offered to them, after they cross from this world.

We have watched people heal and become whole from fires, floods, earthquakes, wars, car accidents and most anything you can think of that could happen to someone to end their earthly life.

We also see people from all walks of life coming together and trying to help each other find their way. They talk to each other and find that they are just as human as the other was. They finally understand that every person that ever walked the earth, was designed by God and given life by God. They now understand to take another person's life is to take away a gift from God and an insult to top it all off. We have seen grown men and women, grab each other to give them a hug and cry tears of joy. They tell each other how sorry they are that they did not see what they see now, when they walked the earth plane. It has been amazing the sites we have witnessed on the other side!

SECTION SIX: WORKING WITH YOUR CREATIVE ANGELS

The Gift of Healing from the Angels

Angel Crystal Grid Work Healing

I have studied Healing Touch and completed all of the levels in this form of healing from 1993 – 1997. I became a Reiki Master/Teacher in 2003. When I was taking each of these classes I knew that there was something else that I would be using with these modalities.

I was shown in late 2002, the, "Angel Crystal Grid Work". This was an amazing type of work. I was given one of the most wonderful gifts to work with. It was the five surgeons, who always appeared once the crystal grid was in place. I also was given a beautiful gift of the liquid healing light that radiated a wonderful blue and white healing light energy. This same light appeared at our Monday meetings when we did healing work.

On January 30, 2003 our monthly Saturday night group meeting also experienced the wonderful gift of the liquid healing ball of energy light. We were told to use this light and replenish ourselves with it when we needed it. There is an abundant supply of this energy light. We were told to come often, to keep this orb of light close to us and use it as much as possible.

This was a wonderful confirmation for me when our group had this experience. The Angels told me, others have had this experience also and know about this light orb of healing. Some are trusted with the light, trusted to only do something good with the light.

The Angels told me,

> "We would not have shown people this if we did not trust that the time was right for it to be used again in this world.
>
> This is the Light Energy and it is a gift from God. It is a God force to be used for the creation of Peace in this world. This will bring about a Nation of Peace. Picture all people in this Light, watch as it changes each person that you put into it.
>
> This is the Healing Light, Prosperity Light, & Peace Light! This Light shines all over the world.
>
> Tranquility ~ Liquid Light
>
> Watch as it grows. As you use it more and more, it will continue to grow stronger and multiply over and over again. It is an endless stream of light. It is never ending. It has an abundant supply for all!
>
> With all of the changes that occur in this world, we ask that you wrap the universe and all that encompasses it, in this Light. Cover it with a beautiful blanket of Light for Protection.

Send protection to the people of this world. God is near, always near and ready to fill everyone's heart with the Light of Love."

The Angels of the Light

Meditation #7: The Light of Abundance

Meditate with the Light of Abundance. Watch it as you put into it what you desire. Picture it moving out into the universe. It is time to allow the light to work for you at this point. Do not keep asking over and over again. Just let the light work the way it is meant to be.

Believe it will return to you, with what you desire. Allow it to be in God's timing. It will return to you with a blessing from God.

What colors do you observe with this light? Keep the light flowing on a steady beam of energy.

Keep focusing on the Light. Watch it as it moves around. Now start to focus on it to the point that you can move it with your mind.

Picture what you are asking for. See it in color format with all of the detail you can put into it.

Make your mind see it wrapped in the blanket of light. Push this light out into the universe.

MEDITATION #7: THE LIGHT OF ABUNDANCE

Watch as the hands of God reach down and pick it up. Make the light move towards what it is that you put out in your desire. Have the light and whatever your desire is, become one with each other. Merge them together.

Watch as the hands of God sends the Light back to you. Once the light is back and circling you, then picture the area around you filled with all of the wonderful healing energy of the Love of God.

Then see your desire manifest right before your eyes. The matter takes shape and your desire is formed.

Practice this meditation on a daily basis. Start with something small to experience a quick start then move up to bigger things.

Remember the Universe is never out of stock of anything you need to improve your life and to help others."

Your band of Angels of Abundance

"Unite together as your Shield of Armor!"

"Love to you and the World!"

ANGEL EXPERIENCES

SECTION SEVEN

SECTION SEVEN: ANGEL EXPERIENCES

"Angels Divine, Angels of Mine"

Beside me you fly

Beside me you fly

Holding my hand you take me afar.

Lighting the way, clearing the Path

Reaching out to hold me and carry me high

Riding that wave up into the sky

You are my Angel, my Angel Divine

That Angel, that Angel of Mine

Madrina ~ April 9, 2009

SECTION SEVEN: ANGEL EXPERIENCES

Last Section ~ Right Now Begins the Rest of your Life

I have noticed that we now have seven sections to this book because the Angels have asked me to add this last one. The number seven is the highest spiritual number. It is always referred to in the Bible. The energy of a SEVEN is telling us to begin to focus inward and find your spiritual understanding. Its vibration is about becoming more silent.

Take time now to rest and find your peace within your own self. When you do this, it will lead you to finding your spiritual being within.

Now that being said, by now hopefully you understand that meditation or being in a prayerful manner will lead you to finding your Angels. Are you still asking how you will know if you are hearing from your Angels or having an experience of any kind with an Angel?

They have asked me to end their book by sharing with you some of my Angel experiences that have occurred over time in my life, as well as other people's Angel experiences. This is so you may recognize your own Angel experiences when they happen.

I will begin this section with my Angel Encounters. I began having some experiences when I was a young child.

I know that I really am not much different than other people with this. It is just that I have been asked to write about it and talk about it in public. This is to help others to become aware of the magnificent help they have in life.

When I was very young I would notice that there were different lights that took shape behind people. These lights would show up near-by when things in life were more challenging, as well as when people were having fun. These lights changed depending on what was happening in people's lives. I also felt the presence of the Angels at various times in my own life.

I know that the Angels followed me to and from school as we walked along the way.

SECTION SEVEN: ANGEL EXPERIENCES

I know that we had them around us as we played. It was something I did not really need to be taught, because for some unknown reason I just knew what they were.

When I went to school I learned more about God and the bible. I knew then what I felt all those years was true.

I know as I learned to drive, I was blessed by God to have these special Angels beside me. Have you ever come to a light, to only have it turn green and for some strange reason you did not go. All of a sudden a car went flying through the intersection and you would have been hit had you gone?

Pay attention to the times when you are running just a little bit late getting to an appointment. You finally get on the road and driving along you see there was an accident on the side of the road that had just happened. You know that if you had just been five or six minutes earlier you would have been in that accident. There are so many times you can place a point in life where an Angel interceded in your life to help you through things.

I know that even when I was in a car accident or the one time a deer came through my windshield, the Angels were there to help me with the situation. Someone either came along to help or I made it home in a strange way and I knew God had sent a messenger to help me.

ANGEL TALK / CHATTING WITH THE ANGELS

The night the deer was at the side of the road, I was driving down a very busy road in Indiana. There where many trucks traveling on this road, at all times of the night. It was a Friday night at about 7:30 p.m. on a chilly October evening. I saw the deer on the side of the road and slowed way down because I figured she was coming across. Instead, the deer turned around and headed up the hill, so I started to go forward again.

Just as I got the speed up to about thirty-five miles per hour she turned, ran and jumped over my car. The problem was the poor thing missed. Her back hoof hit my car and tripped her up. She landed right on the front end of the car. She came right through my windshield. I remember just trying to come to a stop and made sure I had control of the car. I can remember telling God this was quite the joke taking me out with the backend of a deer! That would be a good joke for people to tell!

I closed my eyes just as I saw the deer come through the windshield. I did not want to see the deer hit me. I managed to get my car to a stop and I did not hear any noises, so I opened my eyes. The deer was not in my car as I had imagined I would see. I just sat there for a few minutes trying to get my wits about me.

Suddenly I thought, "Gosh I am going to get hit from behind." I tried to look into my rear view mirror to make sure no one was coming, but my mirror was gone. My glasses were gone also, so I had trouble seeing very far.

SECTION SEVEN: ANGEL EXPERIENCES

By now it was getting pretty dark outside. I looked around and did not see any lights. I looked for a place to pull off the road. There was a driveway right beside my car so I pulled in there. I turned my car off and got out of the car to look at the damage. Just as I turned to look around, a truck was coming up the road from behind me and another one was traveling down the road the other way. I just got back into my car and sat there thinking, "Man that was way too close!"

There was a steady stream of traffic all of a sudden. I just sat there and thanked God for the help. This was before cell phones, and because I was by myself, I did not want to go to a stranger's house to ask for help. Without thinking very much I found that my car still ran. Before I knew it, I had pulled into my driveway, got out of the car and walked into my house where my family was sitting and watching television. I am not sure how I made it home or why I would even think to drive a car without a windshield, but I would not recommend it. I just remember being so cold when I arrived home and I was covered in glass. It was all pretty amazing really!

I looked around to make sure I was really okay and found only a very small cut on my finger. There was deer fur in my steering wheel and glass everywhere. I found my glasses in the back seat on the floor along with my rearview mirror. I called the police to make the report.

I would never have thought to drive home in that condition in my right mind. Somehow that night it worked out. I am safe today. I know the Angels were with me on that drive home.

I was only a block from the back road I took to go home. It was only about a twenty-minute drive. I still do not even remember that drive home. I still find that totally amazing!

Another time I was on my way home from work, I was going around a bend, when I saw a car lose control on the other side of the road. It was coming right at me. I felt my car being turned sideways. I looked and I was right by a driveway, that was wide enough for me to drive my car into sideways. I looked ahead and the car was still coming at me. Suddenly it was turned sideways and stopped just about a paper width in front of my car.

If the driver had gone just a few more inches she would have hit me and then gone into the ditch. She was pretty shaken up and apologized to me. We both just shook our heads in disbelief. We were both able to drive off without a scratch.

My children told me of the times they had a car accident and felt an Angel with them. I know that with teens I could write a whole chapter about the stories of the accidents. We talk about some of them and can not help but think, there was someone with them during that time. There was no way they should have walked away from several of these accidents.

SECTION SEVEN: ANGEL EXPERIENCES

I had talked with my children when I was asked to write this part of the book. They confirmed again, all these years later, that they knew they had help during those times in their lives.

My son Stanley, told me about the time he was driving our tractor. He was going down a very steep hill and the road was covered with ice. He was trying to pull his car out of the ditch. He was heading down the hill and the tractor started to slide. The steering wheel locked up, the brakes were not working and he just kept sliding. Suddenly, the tractor slid sideways, turned into the hillside and stopped his decent down the hill. The road had a big bend in it with a drop off on one side. He was stopped right at that bend.

He told me he felt his Angel with him that day! He said even today he knows God was with him and sent him the Angels to help stop the tractor.

I have to say at this time, that I have had many parents ask me why God was not there when their children were killed in a car accident.

I have asked the Angels and this is the message I received:

"We are going to tell you, God was there and we did come to give our assistance. Humans sadly think God has abandoned them when things are hard to handle in their lives. The loss of a child in any manner is life changing. We can tell you, God was there to help and the Angels continue to help you through your years to cope with this difficult situation.

When your mission is over here as a human, God decides it is time to take you back home again.

He sends the messengers of the Light and brings you home. Your spirit is lifted from the body and the person moves past the obstacles.

It then travels on into the light and is greeted by family and friends. The care never fails and never ends."

       Your Angels of God's Light   May 11, 2009

Angel's Interaction at Transition Time

God has a way of taking care of us, when we most need it. When someone we love passes away, it is one of the most difficult times in our life. We just need to know that God sends the help we need. He provides us with the care and help to heal from this grief.

I have been blessed to be able to help people in their Transition times. I have been a witness to what transpires during the days and hours leading up to the time the spirit actually leaves the body. I have been with several friends as their loved ones have passed or just shortly before. This is a whole different fascinating story in itself, but in this book I will share with you the experiences I have had with the Angels during this time.

SECTION SEVEN: ANGEL EXPERIENCES

Dorothy

Many years before I became more involved in this work, my mother-in-law passed away. I can remember standing in the room only a few hours before, looking at her. I kept getting a feeling things were just not right. I did not want to leave the hospital. I was planning a trip away for the weekend and the doctors told us she was doing better.

I left the hospital and on the way home from my visit with her, I had decided I would not go away. I just did not feel that things were right.

I would just tell the children that we needed to stay home so I could go back up and visit Nana. I went to a friend's house to sit and wait for the children to get off the bus. I received the call to come back to the hospital. I called my husband and told him to head out from work. I then called my sister-in-law and we headed back to the hospital.

We were almost there when I got this feeling that something happened. I could feel the energy of my mother-in-law beside me. I looked at my watch to check the time because I could feel Dorothy leave her body. This would be a confirmation to me if it turned out to be close to the time she passed into spirit.

We arrived at the hospital where the Chaplin met us and took us into a room to tell us that mom had passed. We were taken to her room and I held her hand.

I felt a tremendous peace in the room once I saw her. I just knew she had made it home. I felt a calm and warm feeling come over me. I knew God had sent the Angels to take her home. I also knew I had been sent a message not to go too far away.

Thanks Mom for everything, you are a blessing in my life not just a mother-in-law but a friend!

Cindy's Grandmother

My friend Cindy asked me to put the things that happened with her grandmother in the book.

I will only tell a little of that here because I am working on another book to help with the transition of the spirit and soul. I will have more details later.

Cindy's grandmother is referred to as Granny. She was a wonderful person. I am blessed because I knew her during her lifetime here. She stayed in this life until she was 96 years of age.

During her last few weeks of life we noticed all kinds of changes. She would go back in time thinking she was back at her home when she was younger. She would also be talked to her relatives that were already in spirit. I noticed in the last few days of her life, I could see the Angels

SECTION SEVEN: ANGEL EXPERIENCES

around and lots of her family members from the spirit world were coming and going.

The Angels stood beside Cindy and held her while she held Granny's hand. Then as Granny slipped from her human body into the light, I could see the lights changing more rapidly. Suddenly I watched as the Angels enfolded her spirit being as it lifted from her human body and the room filled with a brilliant light. The Angels looked at me and I could feel the peace in the room. I was told they were taking her spirit home again.

I was so moved by this experience to be able to witness such a miraculous event I was overwhelmed by the gifts and blessing from God.

Still thinking of you Granny!

Joan's Dad

Another friend, Joan told me that her dad was taking a turn for the worse. I decided that I needed to go over and check on her to make sure she was okay. When I arrived at her house and looked in on her dad, I had this feeling I needed to stay the night to help her get some sleep. My Angel was telling me she would need all the sleep she could get. I was told that there would be a lot of commotion over the weekend and she would need her strength.

I was with Joan and her dad the last twenty-four hours before his spirit left his body.

There were many visitors from the spirit world. Everyone was rushing around to make sure we would be okay. They were checking on her dad to prepare him for this journey. The Angel showed up several times during the night and into the next day. I was told, this was to begin the process to prepare his body and his spirit for his transition.

This process must be prepared for the journey home and the groundwork needed to be done ahead of time to make the journey easier for the human person.

We saw so many different lights and the energy in the room was different. The Angels just radiated peace in the room and that energy filled Ralph. You could tell from his breathing that it was his time to go home.

SECTION SEVEN: ANGEL EXPERIENCES

William Barnes

One day I received a phone call from my friend Denise asking if I would go and talk with her grandfather. She told me that he was looking to talk with a minister. The day I arrived at William's house, I met a wonderful person who quickly became my friend. I only knew him a short period of time.

During this time, he made an impact on my life. He asked me to call him Bill. He told me that all of his friends called him that.

A few months had passed since our first visit. I received another phone call. This time they had found that Bill's health had taken a turn. He wanted me to come and talk to him. I went to the hospital. I had to leave him a note because he was not in his room. I found out a few days later he had been moved to a nursing home. I went to visit with him.

I was blessed with the opportunity to talk and pray with Bill. I could feel the Angels and family members from spirit around him. I told him about the Angels and family that were around him. I explained to him to make sure he looked for them when his time came.

He told me he believed in the Angels and afterlife. He said he felt so much more at peace after our prayers. I was able to sit with him a few more times before his spirit went home and each time was a blessing for me. I just wanted to take care of him and make sure he was going to be okay in the process of the transition. He told me he would be just fine. I believed him.

He said he had found a peace. He said he regretted not meeting me sooner. I told him there should be no regrettes! Bill thanked me for being his friend.

He passed into spirit while I was out of town. Before I left I told him. to call to me in the night if he needed me and I would be there for him. I felt him that night and sent out the energy to him. I knew he would be okay. I received the call on my way home that he had passed.

What an awesome man! I Love you Bill, my friend!

I am told the Angels visit during this time, to assist with the people that will be left behind in this world. Then there are Angels that prepare the person leaving.

The Angel of Transition works on being there to lead the person to the other side so they are not alone. This Angel is also known as the Angel of Death, but would rather be called, "The Angel of the Light". This energy leads us to the wonderful, brilliant light awaiting us. It is the light that shines to light the way to our spiritual home.

It has been very interesting and a blessing in my life working with all of these people. It has been an honor to have ministered with each person over the years. It has been an amazing journey helping to prepare them for their next stage of life.

SECTION SEVEN: ANGEL EXPERIENCES

Gail's Angel Experience

I was talking to my friend Gail and she told me she would love it if I would include her Angel experience in this book. You will hear Gail tell of how an Angel helped her with her mother's passing. As she talks about this I can hear the emotion in her voice. She still feels the emotion coming over her as she remembers how she first saw the Angel in her house.

She told me that just before her mother passed into spirit, an Angel came and wrapped its arms around her. This is her story as told to me.

"I was at home alone and on the phone with my mom. I was standing by the window in the kitchen. At 9:10 A.M. I hung up the phone. I walked into the living room and there was a woman standing there. She did not have any wings, but she was so beautiful and perfect.

Every hair on my body stood up and tears began to fall down my face. The woman disappeared and then quickly turned to white light. She moved quickly and went into the hallway.

I called my mom to talk to her about this and she was not sure what it was. She thought maybe it was a spirit. About a week and a half later, my mom passed away.

This energy kept coming back to hold me and wrap her arms around me. I knew she had come to help me with my mom's passing.

I still get chills today talking about this experience. I believe this experience is what lead me to study more about all of this. I know this is why I have started my studies of Mediumship."

Story submitted by: Gail C.

In this story you can tell that this experience has really made a tremendous impact on Gail's life. I know that I can see such a difference in her from the first time that I met her until today. The Angels have given her a blessing that can not be replaced by anything else.

SECTION SEVEN: ANGEL EXPERIENCES

Abuse of the Angels?

I had an interesting conversation with one of my clients who felt that the people, who did this type of work with the Angels or wrote books about the Angels, were telling people to use the Angels for things that they should not be asking for. She felt it was abusing them. She felt that asking the Angels for parking spaces and menial things such as this, was something we should not be doing. She said the Angels have more important things to take care of than this.

I wanted to question the Angels about this, but then I thought that would be bothering them while they did the more meaningful tasks. I was serious about this, because the Angels had told me differently. I have always been told to ask the Angels. They have told me over and over again that it was their privilege to work with us. They said all we need do was to ask them and they would be here for us.

I needed to ask this question so I could have an answer for this type of belief and here is the answer I received:

May 26, 2009

"Oh dear Christine, what a shame it is that people in your world think we are too busy saving the world, to help you on a daily basis. We understand and are not insulted in any way by this belief. We are here tonight to clear this topic of conversation.

We will tell you again that it is our honor to work with your world. We are excited to help the people grow in their spiritual development.

This is one of the very beginning levels of learning and growth. When we answer the little things in life, it teaches that we can be there in the grander scale of life. Walking steadily along your path with our guidance is a glorious thing to see from our view.

There are many plains here and many levels of Angels. We have a battlefield of Angels working on the worldly matters and a battlefield of Angels working on Personal and Spiritual Development.

We understand that the human beings do not want to take advantage of our time. We are honored by this concern at this time. We are the Angels of God's Light and Love. It is once again our honor and duty to help your level of humans learn the highest level of understanding, you can comprehend in this lifetime. It will take many levels of learning to accomplish this.

If it helps you believe we are around by asking us for the simple things in life, then rest assured we are at the helm working on the worldly matters.

One day you will learn you do not have to ask for all of the small things in life because you will understand they are already there for your use.

SECTION SEVEN: ANGEL EXPERIENCES

It is nice at times for us to gift you these wonderful surprises. We do get such delight in all of this.

Believe us then that we are here to surround you with the Godly Light of the Divine Rays of Love. It will protect you throughout your life and send out the Rays for others to absorb.

It is our hope that you will now understand this answer of this nature and travel with us on your journey in life."

> The Guardians of Angels and Light

I would say from this answer that the Angels are helping us grow spiritually when we work with them. I know from my own experiences, I can tell you that I feel I do not have to ask as much for the little things any longer. I have found I believe it is being done without me asking. I have the faith to believe that if something happens, no matter what the outcome, it is for my highest and best in this life.

I will continue to ask the Angels every so often for something like a parking space. This way I can let others see that it works! It is always fun to go somewhere and say I asked the Angels for this and watch it happen.

Shelby and Ethan's Angel Experience

Shelby is my granddaughter, and she can see the Angels. She always talked to us about her experiences and what she watched happen around people. I remember one day when we picked her up from school, I had asked her how her day went. She became so excited! She told me that at lunchtime she was playing on the playground and saw some Angels.

I asked her what they were doing? She started to laugh. I said, "What is so funny?" Shelby looked at me and said, "The Angels were so funny because they were playing soccer on the playground." She said they were laughing and running all over the place. She saw them all the time at school, around the other children, during sports events and many other times.

She saw the Angels around me also. I had talked to her about this asking her if she saw anything. She told me about the one I saw standing right there, so I know for sure she was seeing just what I did.

I was talking to my grandson Ethan about Angels and asked him if he knew about Angels. He said, "Oh grandma everyone has an Angel!" I asked him what his looked like. He laughed and said it looks just like him and likes to do the same things he likes to do.

SECTION SEVEN: ANGEL EXPERIENCES

He told me he sees and talks to his Angel all the time. He says the Angel plays with him. Ethan thought I was silly for asking him about the Angels because he knows I see them.

Shelby and Ethan told me, that the Angels just wanted everyone to be safe, play and have fun.

It is so cute to talk to each of the children, and hear their stories and experiences about the Angels in their lives. I just can not wait to hear Quintin, my other grandson's stories one day, when he gets old enough to tell me all about them. My goal is to help each of my grandchildren remember they have these Angels in their lives and to help other children to learn about their own Angels.

God Sends People into My Life

All throughout my life people have come to me to talk about things in their life. I always seemed to have the right words come into my mind to say, to help them. If I did not get the words, I knew I was just supposed to sit and listen. I feel like these are God inspired words and actions given to me by the Angels to help others. I believe this is one of the reasons I am a minister today.

Little by little over the years I have met people who have had experienced the Angels in many different ways. I have become friends with many of these people. It just amazes me what has happened in my life since I started to write with the Angels.

The following are just a few examples of how I met some of these friends.

Saturday Night Meetings

I have been helping some friends over the years learn more about Angels and they have had some very interesting experiences. Through these experiences I felt I needed to start a gathering with a group of people who could work together to develop a higher vibration.

SECTION SEVEN: ANGEL EXPERIENCES

Connie is a friend that I have known for over thirty years.

Her mom was involved with groups that learned all kinds of interesting things about the Angels and Spirits. We did fun things over the years to grow and learn what we could about these things. We stayed friends and our bond grew stronger over the years. We started going to her mother's house and some of the family came over. We would do meditation and other interesting things.

When that faded away, we found it was time to sit together for an hour each week and do a meditation. She found when I guided a meditation to fly with the Angels, she would get wonderful adventures with them. She has had some very insightful experiences that have helped her with her life. These experiences have guided her to study healing and mediumship. Connie traveled with me as my helper to the home parties I started to do in the mid 1990's. I worked with her over the years teaching her the things I learned in the many classes I took. Connie is a wonderful person and a very dear friend.

I am very proud of her for all of the accomplishments in her life! Thanks for being my friend!

David was brought into my life when I was invited to come to his sister's house to do a home party. David could see and hear the spirits I was seeing. We met again several years later at his house where I met his family to help the trapped spirits that collected at his house. I taught him what the Angels had showed me, to help these spirits to move on.

ANGEL TALK / CHATTING WITH THE ANGELS

We decided it was time for us to start a group of like-minded people to sit to do meditation, and listen to what the Angels wanted us to hear. We met different people over time that have come and gone from this Saturday night group, but we still remain strong about seven years later. Connie, Cindy, her husband Paul, Tom and Laney, David and Denise, my husband Stan and I, are working to help spirits move to the other side. We are also learning together from the Angels and the Master Teacher in our journey to the other side, channeling the Angels, worked with healing, and sending out energy to bring peace to the world.

I am told that others meet in the same manner. One day we should do a convention of like-minded people. I am told that we would be amazed at how much we have learned from the Angels, which are very similar. The Angels also told me that we will continue to grow and work for the lighting of the world. To teach others how to sit in meditation and grow spiritually.

I am told that there is more to this meeting. We will continue to hold the energy for world peace. We are sometimes shown things that will happen in the world just before they happen. We are told to pray and send out the energy for each person involved.

This group was formed to work on our spiritual path but it was to help the Universe heal and bring about many changes in the world.

SECTION SEVEN: ANGEL EXPERIENCES

Monday Night Class

I met Tammy and Pam by doing a reading for them at a friend's house. They both lived near my house. I had never met them before the day of their scheduled readings. After this reading we exchanged emails since they lived near me and we kept in touch.

Debbie became a part of my life in a really wild way. She was testing for her Mediumship papers at the church I was attending and I was going for my certification. When we finished working, I talked with her and found out that she only lived about ten minutes from our house. We went to church an hour away from our homes. I had never met her before, and this was at the time I kept feeling I needed to start a Monday night class.

I was asked to do a class for people, so they could learn about communicating with the Angels and Spirit. I asked Tammy, Pam and Debbie if they would like to come and join with me to practice these things.

It turned out to be a class where I was teaching what was given to me over the years and so our Monday night group was formed many years ago.

Tammy is someone I call an Earth Angel because she seems to know just the right things to say to people and is always helping others. Through her studies she has found she writes with the Angels.

Pam had some very interesting experiences in our meditations that lead her to believe she could work with her Angels also.

Carol came to our class one night as a guest and we all gravitated to her right away and asked her to come back again. We found she had been writing with the Angels and talking to them for awhile. She is such a blessing in our lives.

I am shown this group is a wonderful experience for me. I became a teacher of the Spiritual journey. I am to continue to help each person grow on their journey, in the manner needed , to work in their own life.

SECTION SEVEN: ANGEL EXPERIENCES

The United Spiritualist of the Christ Light Church.

I have met wonderful people, when I found my first Spiritualist church in Cincinnati, Ohio called, the United Spiritualists of the Christ Light Church. (U.S.C.L.). This began my major life transformation when I found a church that thought and believed just like I had, for all of my life.

The first people I met were Rev. Danny, Alison, Barb, Earl, Rev. Rose, Jane, Judy, Theresa and Tom. Each one has touched my life over the years.

Rev. Rose Vanden Eynden is now a wonderful friend, author, healer, teacher and a blessing to my life. We have worked together many times at church. There was one time she needed someone to work with her on a radio show and she asked me to do the show with her. We did an Angel Message event on the radio.

We always have so much fun working together. We have talked many times about the Angels and our work for them. She was inspired by the Angels to write books and her book about the Angels is called: **Metatron: Invoking the Angels of God's Presence.** It is a fantastic book inspired by the Angel Metatron.

There are so many people that I have met at USCL over the years. I thank each and every one of them for being a part of my life, for the inspiration and support they have all given me.

Camp Chesterfield

Camp Chesterfield is a Spiritual learning center for those studying Mediumship, Metaphysical Studies, and studying for Ordination. I met so many people at Camp Chesterfield while studying to become a minister, and during my journey to becoming an Ordained Minister, I learned and grew. There are so many people that traveled this journey of studies with me. I would have to write pages to mention all of the people who touched my life during the years at camp. I would like to thank everyone for all the blessings and love they have shared with me over the wonderful years of studying at Camp Chesterfield. There was always a welcome mat out for me when I arrived, Mary Beth made sure of that. I will always have fond memories of my journey.

Mike and Susan are teachers and my friends. They gave me opportunities to work at their church Progressive Spiritualist Church in Indianapolis, Indiana. They taught me in ways they do not realize. They have helped me today with my ministry. They taught me what ministorial work was all about. I watched them with their congregation, their determination and I learned so much learned.

SECTION SEVEN: ANGEL EXPERIENCES

Spiritualist Church of Light and Hope

Throughout my journey at Camp Chesterfield, I met Doug. We became friend. He wanted to open a church in our area. I needed to go through this opportunity to grow and become stronger so I could teach others.

This was difficult for me because there came a time when I accepted the position as the Assistant Pastor of the church. By doing so, I had to become less involved at the USCL. I had many friends at this church and this was a difficult decision. I found this was something I felt I was being guided by God to do. So that is what I did.

We worked hard at this task. Over the years I found that I loved being a minister. I cared so much for our congregation. I wanted to give the best to them, and help them grow spiritually. I met so many people. Each one has brought many special blessings into my life.

I kept up with my friends at USCL. When it looked like this church was going through changes and was struggling to stay open, I started talking with them on ways we could merge the churches.

Sometimes life is not about what we want, but what we need, at the time. This happens even when we can not see what we need at that time in our life.

In May of 2009, Doug told me our church would be closing in two weeks. When I heard this news, it was a very sad day for me. I had a very difficult time with this. I knew this was hard for Doug.

Sometimes you need to go with the flow and allow things to happen in your life. This allows for the new journey to begin, and opportunities to open up for you.

I did not want to quit being a minister. I felt that if you worked on something, then put it out in the Universe for God to work on, it would happen if it is meant to happen. I do not feel that you can always put something away until later if and when the right time comes. Sometimes the right time does not come again.

When you have momentum on something this important, you take it and you keep it moving forward. I also know that many times there is burn out on things that are not happening the way you planned it to happen.

I walked around lost for days. I wondered why I had been guided in this direction. I hated the idea of letting this go! I wondered what our congregation would do from here. I thought about it constantly.

I could only hope that our church helped as many people as we could.

SECTION SEVEN: ANGEL EXPERIENCES

I finally had to let go of the worry about this and the lost feelings. I knew worry was not a good thing to do when looking for answers.

Doug had told me that he felt that in a few years maybe time would give the church a new strength and life. That was not meant to be.

Rev. Douglas Balzer passed into spirit just before this book went to press. I send my heartfelt prayers to his family, as they move forward in their lives.

New Adventures

I once again turned to my faith in God to find my way in life. I prayed about this and I received this answer:

May 20, 2009

"Dear Child,

You are being given a golden opportunity at this time in life. You now have an open door of opportunity to begin again. It is a new journey. This is the beginning of where you will need to be for the next phase in your life, and the work for God. Pick your energy up and move forward with the flow that will follow this time. Begin to look ahead. Follow the light and you will see your way clearly again.

Travel will come for you and words will be given, to help others with the way of your world.

Take your light out, shine it for the world to see. It will come back to you. This is a fresh new way of life."

Your Angels of God's Words of life

The words from the Angels hit home hard. I felt the church was supposed to close at this time. I found my peace in it all.

SECTION SEVEN: ANGEL EXPERIENCES

There were many others that thought as I did about the church and held the idea of a Spiritualist church to heart. They wanted to see it continue to grow. I had several people from our church, who wanted to get together to plan on where to go from here.

Everyone came up with ideas. There were several things brought up to do from here. I told them I would be going back to USCL. I had been talking with several of my friends from the church already, about the two congregations merging. I would commit to helping them grow. We needed to put the momentum and determination into this church. We could become strong from here, and see where it took us. They agreed to come along and help with this task.

We also decided to start a group that would meet and grow together. This group has become family. We continue to meet after church on Sundays, and then once a month we get together to talk about our Spiritual path.

I would like to thank the following people: Sherri, Angel, Jenny, Connie, Rose, Fran, Norma, Rick, Penny, Andie, Mike, Tanya, Sarah, Ida Lee, Kevin, Brenda, Sara G., David, Denise, my husband Stan and my children for helping me get through a time of change in the balance of my life, and helping to bring the light to so many.

I can say the merger of the two churches happened, just not the way I thought it would.

That is a good thing. I feel that if you let God take the reins, it works out much better than anyone could have ever dreamed.

Remember, it is a constant thing in life to try to let go and let God! Is it not?

I am always happy to look up and see someone from the church come in on Sunday at USCL. It is like home now. Everyone has been so welcoming. It is refreshing to see so many dedicated people in the church on Sundays. I feel like we have a new chance to grow as a strong Spiritualist family. I look forward to the Spiritual teachings that Jesus and many other Master Teachers have taught all throughout time.

There are so many teachers that we have been given to work with. They all have so much to teach us. That is the greatest thing about Spiritualism. It allows us to explore and study with so many great teachers from our past. It is an awesome religion. I have found my home. I feel at peace with the world.

This is a wonderful experience, there are several ministers at the USCL that will all work together on the spiritual side of the church to help it grow. We work with the dedicated board members, to help rebuild our Spiritualist foundation to help others in their spiritual development.

It does not matter if your life is in balance, or if it is out of balance, the Angels will fly with you.

SECTION SEVEN: ANGEL EXPERIENCES

They will bring in the people who are needed to help you get through it all. You will come out stronger than ever before.

As I look back over this last year, I am amazed at how much of the Angel teachings have been a part of my life. They have taught me about remaining in a balance in life, and keeping peace in my heart. So much has happened all year, all the way up to this book being ready to go to press. I am including the following to help those going through difficulties.

The most recent thing that came up in my life was just a few weeks ago. I found out many things I thought I knew about a person, was not true, and this person was a friend. There is so much unfolding about things which have transpired over the last few years. I am being told about things this person said, about me to others, that I know as a fact to be a lie. It is hard to confront someone who is now in spirit.

I know for the last few weeks, I have thought so much about all that I am hearing. I felt like my mind would just not be able to handle all of the processing that was happening.

It is amazing to me about life. I did so much thinking about this that I actually started to fall and walk into doors. The last fall just a few weeks ago, hurt the most. I broke my rib, my arm and bruised my body in the fall. I was hurting pretty bad.

I heard myself say, "Why am I beating myself up so much over all of this?" Once I heard this, it was as if I woke up!

I have also heard news about my sister Kathy, who has cancer. It has now spread to her brain. She is so special to me. This is a very difficult time for my family. I have turned it over to God. I am sending out healing energy and prayers to my family.

There are problems with my computer running so slow. The manuscript for this book is messing up, when I download it trying to get it ready for print. That makes so much sense with all that is going on. Computers are run on electricity and electricity is energy. When the energy around you is wild and crazy, then sometimes electrical things go crazy also.

So much is happening all around. I know it is time to take a deep breath and allow the peace to flow again. I said this is enough. I found a peace inside myself over all the hurt I was feeling. I also found a peace about the friendship and the lies that were spread about me, that I could never go back and undo.

I just sit back tonight and tell God I am putting it all in his lap. I see the white light coming down to me and taking everything from me.

I see the Ball of White Light enter the room, and surround me and my family. I instantly feel the peace and love of God enfold me.

SECTION SEVEN: ANGEL EXPERIENCES

I am sending this feeling out to my family and all of the others in the world suffering or going through difficulties in life.

I find this week as I look at everything in a different perspective, I am processing things as they happen. Before I know, it things begin to work themselves out, right in front of me. I suddenly am able to see things in a different way and begin to heal inside. I know that God is around me, and helping me with these situations.

Sometimes in life things seem so unfair. When these times come, you have to turn it over to God.

Come to terms with it. Believe that there is a reason. You will learn something from it. Then go on with life, in a much better frame of mind.

I asked the Angels for some answers about all of this. This is the answer they gave me:

December 10, 2009

"Dear sweet child of God,

We come tonight to bring comfort and joy to you. We hear that you are sad from this loss. We feel your disappointment in a friend.

Understand that sometimes people are misguided by others, and find that they are caught up in things in life. They find that they are also lost.

In this circumstance you must believe, that you will find a way to forgive and move forward again in life.

Most important, there might never be a true reason why you walked this path and got hurt in the process.

You blessed many in this path, and helped many more. That is what you will now be asked to stay focused on.

Where is your heart and intentions? Where will you go from here? You can never move forward carrying the unsettled feeling inside.

We ask that you find forgiveness. You will then find your own peace.

So many times, people get caught up in others discomfort in life. When someone is so unsettled in life, they have a need to bring others down.

Your light shines bright, so others will feel they need to put your light out. Do not allow this. Light your lamp and let it shine.

If others want to believe the lies brought about by others, that is something they will do with or without your worries.

SECTION SEVEN: ANGEL EXPERIENCES

Move forward and always bless each person along the way. Know that you are doing what is right. You are following God's will and doing God's work.

We send many blessings to you and your family at this time. God holds you all in his arms, and will continue to dry the tears. We will fly beside your sister, and keep her from the worries. We hold her, and carry her on a distant journey in the next phase of life.

God sees all that is. God is happy with your work and your ways. Continue to reach out and touch others with kindness. The blessings will continue to shine from your heart center to others.

We have been teaching you these lessons, over the years. You are learning along the way, so you are able to adapt to them to help others in their growth processes."

Your Angels of Divine Love and Understanding

I share these stories of my life with each of you to let you see how life can flow. It amazes me all the time how things work in life, with God at the reins.

As you can see from my life, once the Angels become a part of your life, they make sure you are aware of them. They continue to bring more people and experiences into your life. You will find these people have had experiences which will help you along the way.

I will continue to meet people who will touch me. I hope that I can always give back in return. I know right now in my life, I have the best friends and family that anyone could ever ask for.

Angel's Ending Comments

December 3, 2009

It is funny how God works in your life, if you just take a few minutes to stop in your day-to-day activities to pay attention to these types of things.

The Angels say,

> "When doors open and doors close, you will be led to others who will help you on your journey, and to those whom you will help on their journey. It is a balance in life. When the balance swings in one direction, creating an imbalance, then expect changes to occur to bring about a new balance again.
>
> Your life is just like an amusement park. You are either on the merry-go-round riding round and round, never moving forward, stuck in the same rut. Or you choose to ride the roller coaster where you fly through life up and down you go, and around the bends. Before you know it, you have come to the end of your ride, without knowing how fast you rode it.

SECTION SEVEN: ANGEL EXPERIENCES

There are other times, you choose to be a spector, just standing on the sides, watching all the fun. Choosing to not join in.

Find your purpose in life, no matter how simple it feels to you. Find the joy in your life, no matter how sad you feel.

Find the peace in your life, no matter how out of sorts you may seem to feel.

Decide the ticket you purchased for this lifetime, is worth it! Live your life like you just paid a billion dollars for the opportunity to live. Then enjoy every moment so as not to waste any time regretting that you may have spent too much time trying to work on your life."

Blessing and Joy from the Angels above who are honored to be a part of this journey in your lifetime.

"Come along for the ride of your lifetime! Fly with the Angels!"

This journey in my life now brings me to the finishing touches of this book for the Angels. I am finding that I am moving forward with the next stage just as the Angels said.

Sometimes, it is still hard to believe that I hear from the Angels in the manner that I do. It is also hard at times, to follow what I hear for myself, but I continue to listen and learn.

I do know that there is so much guidance here in this world to help with our life. I know the difference between what I hear from my own brain and what I hear from the Angels to write.

I normally get some confirmation from my friends, when they tell me the exact thing the Angels have told me over time. This is always fun!

Actually it is pretty amazing the differences I feel when the Angels come close. There is a light buzzing that comes in the air. I feel a tingling in the back of my neck when they come close. I get a lighter feeling inside my head. Then I notice that my eyes start to soften the focus of my sight. I am unaware of what is going on around me. I cannot feel much of myself. Time has no meaning.

If my husband comes into the room while I am typing and asks me a question, I do not hear him right away. Then I seem to feel startled, and not sure of where I am for a few minutes.

I continue to work on keeping my ears and eyes open, for all the possibilities in life. I have found a new excitement over all that is out there waiting for me. I look forward to all of my wonderful adventures in life.

As I read over this book, I realize that most of it was written directly from the Angels.

SECTION SEVEN: ANGEL EXPERIENCES

I changed the font for what was written in this book from my notebooks. As I typed, I began to notice, that I was still writing the words the Angels were putting into my head.

Wow! The Angels did it again just today February 27, 2010! I received an email today from a publisher that told me to send this book to CreateSpace.com! I asked for guidance on where to send this manuscript, since I was having so much trouble doing self publishing myself. Today in my e-mail, was the mail from a publishing company! It is really amazing!

Thank You so much my dear sweet Angels for the guidance, love and support you have given my family and me through this time in our lives! You have let us know that God is good, and is working in our lives!

I would like to say, thank you to each person who reads this book and shares the information with others. It is my hope that through this journey with the Angels, you find yourself, and your Spiritual path in life.

"Shine On"

Shine Bright, Shine Bright and Fly Along, Fly Along!

Sing a Song, Sing a Song!

Shine again our dear ones, Shine again!

Bring along a smile or two, Bring along a smile!

Hold out your Hands to receive your reward!

See the shining star just for you!

Shine on dear stars of God

Shine on!

Madrina   May 26, 2009

SECTION SEVEN: ANGEL EXPERIENCES

The Angels asked me to end with this statement from them:

> "This is not a book of false hope. We ask that you think about what is said here. Then take time to find new answers and the new keys to life, within your own self.
>
> We send courage, friendship, love and knowledge. We ask that you now take action and move forward in life. It does not matter if you think you are falling. Use the courage to keep going forward. Use the knowledge to make life happen for you in your own fashion, to fit your life in your own mold.
>
> Do not let others stop you from moving forward. Sometimes people of this world do not let themselves be seen for who they are. Use the love we teach about, to guide you to see people for their truth. Then you will experience the divine friendship that is another wonderful gift from our God.
>
> We tell you this Christine, and all the others who are touched by our words. It is now time to move on to start the Angel's Journey of God's Love and Light. It is time, that you begin the travels to teach others the possibility of living a better life through God's Blessings of Love."

Your Angels of Divine Purpose and God's Blessings.

I believe the Angels have come to fight a battle for God, we are asked to come along. Will you come along for the ride? Did you purchase your ticket to life?

"Open your eyes and ears

pay close attention to your call!"

Can We Ignore God's Call Any Longer?

Answer your call and begin your journey today!

SECTION SEVEN: ANGEL EXPERIENCES

The next few pages are empty for you to use for practice.

Begin your own Angel Talk!

ANGEL TALK / CHATTING WITH THE ANGELS

REFERRALS

Christine Sabick: www.radiantbeginnings.com

Christine's new site will give more details as it grows.

Blogs, Facebook and Twitter coming soon!

Stan Sabick: Norwood Custom Glass: 2501 Norwood Ave.

Norwood, Ohio 45212

www.norwoodcustomglass.com

Gary Hopkins: www.findingsource.com

Rose Vanden Eynden: www.vandeneynden.biz

www.vandeneynden.biz/blog -- Read Rose's blog, STANDING BETWEEN THE WORLDS

Do you Twitter? Follow Rose: http://twitter.com/RoseofAvalon

SPIRITUALIST ORGANIZATIONS IN THE UNITED STATES*

Indiana Association of Spiritualists
Camp Chesterfield
P.O. Box 132
Chesterfield, Indiana 46017
765-378-0235
http://www.campchesterfield.net

Lily Dale Assembly
5 Melrose Park
Lily Dale, NY 14752
716-595-08721
http://www.lilydaleassembly.com

The National Spiritual Alliance
P.O. Box 88
Lake Pleasant, MA 01347
http://www.thenationalspiritualallianceinc.org.

National Spiritualist Association of Churches
General Offices
P.O. Box 217
Lily Dale, NY 14752
716-595-2000
http://www.nsac.org

SPIRITUALIST ORGANIZATIONS

Progressive Spiritualist Church - Rev. Susan Mellot & Rev. Mike Mellot
2201 E. 54th St.
Indianapolis, Indiana 46220   -   http://www.progressivespiritualist.net

United Spiritualists of the Christ Light
4412 Carver Woods Drive, Suite 204
Blue Ash, OH 45242
http://www.uscl.org

Universal Spiritualist Association
4905 West University Avenue
Muncie, IN 47304-3460
765-286-0601
http://www.spiritualism.org

This is not a comprehensive list of Spiritualist Organizations in the United States. It does not include any international organizations.

If you would like more information, please contact the organization itself.

Recommended Reading

Christine Sabick: has her second book coming 2011, check with

"COSMIC OPERATOR"

Real life stories from a Medium about the experiences from the Spirit side of life and how they interact with family and friends in the living to bring about healing and to show their love.

Gary Hopkins: To get a copy of Gary's book
"THE MASTER WITHIN"
Please go to: http://www.lulu.com/content/4885824

Rose Vanden Eynden's books, available at all major bookstores:

** "SO YOU WANT TO BE A MEDIUM?" A DOWN TO EARTH GUIDE

** "METATRON: INVOKING THE ANGEL OF GOD'S PRESENCE"

** "ASK A MEDIUM: ANSWERS TO YOUR FREQUENTLY ASKED QUESTIONS ABOUT THE SPIRIT WORLD"